From Strength to Strength

From Strength to Strength

The First Half Century of the Formative Age of the Bahá'í Era

Eunice Braun

Bahá'í Publishing Trust • Wilmette, Illinois 60091

Copyright © 1978 by the
National Spiritual Assembly of the
Bahá'ís of the United States

World Rights Reserved

Library of Congress Cataloging in Publication Data

Braun, Eunice, 1918-
  From strength to strength.

    1. Bahaism—History—20th century.   I.   Title.
BP330.B7   297'.89'0904   78-9424
ISBN 0-87743-125-6

Designed by John Solarz

Printed in the United States of America

The Cause of God, impelled by the mighty forces of life within it, must go on from strength to strength, increasing in size and developing greater and greater powers for the accomplishment of God's purpose on earth.

The Universal House of Justice

Contents

Preface	ix
THE CLOSE OF THE HEROIC AGE	1
The Passing of 'Abdu'l-Bahá	1
Three Divine Charters	2
THE OPENING OF THE FORMATIVE AGE	
(FIRST EPOCH 1921-1944)	5
The Guardianship	5
The First Steps of the Administrative Order	6
Tribulation and Triumph	8
Persian and American Ties	9
The First To Arise	11
Between Wars in Europe	13
The Far East	17
The Passing of the Greatest Holy Leaf	18
The Mother Temple of the West	20
America before the First Seven Year Plan	21
Early Proclamation and Teaching Efforts	21
Publication before the First Seven Year Plan	22
The Promulgation of the Divine Plan	25
The First Seven Year Plan (1937-1944)	25
The First Centenary of the Faith	28
THE SECOND EPOCH OF THE FORMATIVE AGE	
(1944-1963)	31
The Aftermath of the War	31
The Formation of the United Nations	32
The Second Seven Year Plan (1946-1953)	33
A God-Given Mandate	33
Ten National Plans Circle the World	35
The African Campaign	38

Developments at the World Center	39
Appointment of the International Bahá'í Council	40
Appointment of the Hands of the Cause of God	41
A New Plan Foreshadowed	42
The Holy Year and the Great Jubilee	43
The Ten Year World Crusade (1953-1963)	45
The Passing of Shoghi Effendi	47
The Hands of the Cause of God as Chief Stewards	48
The Election of the International Bahá'í Council	49
The Historic First Election of The Universal House of Justice	50
The Bahá'í World Congress, London (April 28-May 2, 1963)	51
THE THIRD EPOCH OF THE FORMATIVE AGE	53
A New, Nine Year Plan	53
Worldwide Proclamation	54
Appointment of the Continental Boards of Counselors	56
Midpoint of the Nine Year Plan	57
Oceanic and Continental Conferences (1970-1971)	58
The Teaching Journeys of the Hand of the Cause of God Amatu'l-Bahá Rúḥíyyih <u>Kh</u>ánum	59
The Conclusion of the Nine Year Plan	60
The Establishment of the International Teaching Center in the Holy Land	63
God's Holy Purpose for Mankind	64
Notes	65

Preface

This brief history of the Formative Age of the Bahá'í Faith was written at the request of The Universal House of Justice and will be included in a forthcoming edition of *The Bahá'í World*. It is dedicated to all Bahá'ís whose lives have been woven into the tapestry of this half century of service to the Faith of Bahá'u'lláh, and to those who will arise today and tomorrow to give of their love and devotion to future victories in the ''unfolding life of the Cause of God.''

EUNICE BRAUN

The Close of the Heroic Age

THE PASSING OF 'ABDU'L-BAHÁ

Early on a November morning in 1921, with darkness on the Mountain of God, and on the slopes of Haifa below, 'Abdu'l-Bahá's earthly life ended. The Heroic Age of the Cause of God was drawing to a close, "that primitive period in which its Founders had lived, in which its life had been generated, in which its greatest heroes had struggled and quaffed the cup of martyrdom...."[1] Through the provisions of His Will and Testament 'Abdu'l-Bahá had forged the vital link that would forever connect the Heroic Age with the Formative Age of the Faith of Bahá'u'lláh, a transitional stage that Shoghi Effendi said "must in the fullness of time reach its blossom and yield its fruit in the exploits and triumphs that are to herald the Golden Age of the Revelation of Bahá'u'lláh."[2]

The Heroic Age of the Faith had begun on May 23, 1844, in Shíráz, Persia, with the call of the Báb, the youthful Prophet-Herald of the Bahá'í Faith. During His brief, turbulent Ministry thousands of His followers were put to death. Two years after the Báb had been martyred in the public square of Tabríz on July 9, 1850, Bahá'u'lláh Himself was arrested and cast into the Síyáh-Chál, a subterranean dungeon in Ṭihrán. He was the Promised One of all ages for Whom the Báb had prepared the way and given His life, and for Whom the world had been waiting for thousands of years. Forty years of exile and imprisonment were in store for Bahá'u'lláh, during which the full import and grandeur of His Mission would gradually unfold.

The first decade of Bahá'u'lláh's exile, in 'Iráq, was marked by the revelation of the Kitáb-i-Íqán (The Book of Certitude) and the Hidden Words, two outstanding contributions to the world's re-

1

ligious literature.'"³ On the eve of His forced departure for Constantinople, in April 1863, Bahá'u'lláh made an open declaration of His Mission to His close followers in the Garden of Riḍván outside Baghdád. During the five years of His Turkish exile, spent mostly in Adrianople, Bahá'u'lláh revealed powerful Tablets to the rulers and religious leaders of East and West. For Bahá'u'lláh, His family, and faithful followers this was a period of increasing tribulation stirred up by an envious half brother, Mírzá Yaḥyá, who labored to create doubt and division among the believers and to plant suspicion in the minds of government officials.

Five years after Bahá'u'lláh's incarceration in the prison-city of 'Akká in 1868, He revealed His Book of Laws, the Kitáb-i-Aqdas (The Most Holy Book).[4] Shortly after His passing on May 29, 1892, the Book of His Covenant, written entirely in His own hand, was unsealed and read. It disclosed that His eldest Son, 'Abdu'l-Bahá (known as the Master) had been appointed the Center of His Covenant and Interpreter of His Revelation. This ignited flames of jealousy and rebellion in the heart of 'Abdu'l-Bahá's half brother Muḥammad-'Alí, a fire that would rage throughout the Master's life and extend into the early years of Shoghi Effendi's ministry. But the Covenant of Bahá'u'lláh had the power to protect His faithful followers from all the forces that would arise in the future to mar the purity of His Faith or to split its ranks. *"'So firm and mighty is this Covenant,'* 'Abdu'l-Bahá affirmed, *'that from the beginning of time until the present day no religious Dispensation hath produced its like.'"*[5]

THREE DIVINE CHARTERS

Toward the close of His life Bahá'u'lláh revealed the Tablet of Carmel, the first of three Divine Charters within the framework of which the Cause of God would unfold.[6] This Charter provided both the impetus and the authority for the development of the World Center in Haifa, as the spiritual focus of the worldwide Bahá'í community and the "heart and nerve-center" of the administrative order.[7] Thus it was ordained that Mount Carmel would one day become the seat of the supreme administrative body, The Universal House of Justice.

The Closing of the Heroic Age

During 1916 and 1917 'Abdu'l-Bahá revealed the second of the Divine Charters, the Tablets of the Divine Plan.[8] This charter for the promulgation of the Faith throughout the world conferred the primary responsibility for its discharge upon the North American Bahá'í community. The third and last of the Divine Charters, the Will and Testament of 'Abdu'l-Bahá, written by His own hand during a period in which He was under great personal danger, is the charter for the World Order of Bahá'u'lláh.[9] It is a document that had both immediate and future application. Shoghi Effendi wrote of it: "We must trust to time, and the guidance of God's Universal House of Justice, to obtain a clearer and fuller understanding of its provisions and implications."[10] It gave immediate authority for the development of the administrative institutions of the Faith. This document, "unique in the annals of the world's religious systems," assured the continuing unity and integrity of the Faith through the appointment of Shoghi Effendi, eldest grandson of 'Abdu'l-Bahá, as Guardian of the Faith of Bahá'u'lláh.[11] It described how The Universal House of Justice ordained by Bahá'u'lláh would be elected and the relationship this supreme institution would have to the Guardianship and to the secondary Houses of Justice (National Spiritual Assemblies). It called for the appointment and outlined the duties of the Hands of the Cause of God, stressed the supreme authority of the Kitáb-i-Aqdas, and warned of the danger and evil of Covenant-breaking. It made teaching the Cause the chief cornerstone of faith.

The Opening of the Formative Age
(First Epoch 1921-1944)

THE GUARDIANSHIP

We stand in the shadow of Shoghi Effendi's thirty-six years of Guardianship, too near to see fully the towering heights of his achievement. Even less, perhaps, can we comprehend the staggering effect that his appointment as Guardian of the Cause of God had upon this youth of twenty-four years. He was attending Oxford University to prepare himself to serve the Faith through mastery of the English language. For two years prior to this he had served as the constant companion and secretary of 'Abdu'l-Bahá. The Hand of the Cause of God Amatu'l-Bahá Rúḥíyyih Khánum, Shoghi Effendi's wife and companion for twenty years, gives us in her book *The Priceless Pearl* a moving insight into the effect of this appointment, coupled with the loss of his beloved Grandfather, upon his pure and sensitive nature.[1]

Aided by Bahíyyih Khánum, the sister of 'Abdu'l-Bahá known as the Greatest Holy Leaf, Shoghi Effendi took immediate steps to rally the Bahá'ís around the world. Within a few weeks he had made contact with the High Commissioner of Palestine, appealed to the Persian believers for steadfastness, written to Bahá'ís in the Far East, and penned a deeply moving letter to the Bahá'ís of North America, in which he recalled the Master's deep trust in the believers there. Soon afterward the British Mandatory Government officially recognized Shoghi Effendi as the head of the Bahá'í Faith.

Brought low by grief and fatigue and by the renewal of vicious attacks from ever-watchful Covenant-breakers, the youthful Shoghi Effendi withdrew from the Holy Land in April 1922, seeking respite in the mountains of Europe. It was a period of "communion with himself and his destiny," a time to marshall his strength.² Later he returned to the Holy Land, "with renewed hope and vigor," to shoulder the unprecedented burden of the Guardianship.³ Messages to Assemblies and to individual Bahá'ís began to flow from his pen—a fresh stream that would become a mighty river in the years to come. During his first year as Guardian he wrote scores of letters to Bahá'ís throughout the world. They were messages of vision and hope, calling the believers to bend their efforts toward Bahá'u'lláh's "great Purpose for mankind."⁴

THE FIRST STEPS OF THE ADMINISTRATIVE ORDER

Though Shoghi Effendi clearly envisaged the work of raising the administrative structure, the Bahá'ís, at the time, only dimly understood the task before them. But the great majority of them loved and trusted this *"priceless pearl"* bestowed upon them by 'Abdu'l-Bahá.⁵ Under the loving guidance of their Guardian, the believers around the world began to lay the foundations of the administrative order with the far goal of erecting The Universal House of Justice, ordained by Bahá'u'lláh and delineated in the Will and Testament of the Master.

Shoghi Effendi, "true brother" to every devoted Bahá'í,⁶ patiently outlined the manner in which local and national Assemblies should be elected and function, as well as the spiritual qualities which their members would need in order to assure success. He stressed the loving, frank spirit of consultation that must underlie every effort. Before the close of his second year as Guardian he had sent detailed guidelines on building the Mother Temple of the West in Wilmette, Illinois; stressed the importance of the Bahá'í Fund; given standards for publishing activities; encouraged the holding of summer schools; and outlined the pattern of committee work.

Raising and guiding the Assemblies was to receive the greater part of Shoghi Effendi's attention for sixteen years. But he never let the Bahá'ís lose sight of the main goal: "to bury our cares and teach the Cause, delivering far and wide this Message of Salvation to a sorely-stricken world." This was the "most urgent" of all obligations, the purpose for which the Divine institutions were being raised.⁷ With all the practical work to be done, personal character was the essential foundation: "Nothing but the abundance of our actions, nothing but the purity of our lives and the integrity of our characters, can . . . establish our claim that the Bahá'í spirit is in this day the sole agency that can translate a long-cherished ideal into an enduring achievement."[8]

In 1921 only a scattering of local Assemblies and Bahá'í centers existed throughout North America, Europe, the Caucasus, India, Persia, the Near East, and Australasia. Bahá'u'lláh Himself had sent traveling teachers to carry His Message abroad. 'Abdu'l-Bahá had called upon Eastern and Western believers, "*heralds of the Covenant*," to make teaching journeys.[9] Now, gradually, the first National Spiritual Assemblies were established: the British Isles, Germany and Austria, and India and Burma in 1923; Egypt and Sudan in 1924; the United States and Canada in 1925; 'Iráq in 1931; Persia and Australia and New Zealand in 1934. They were like beacon lights around the world connected to the powerful dynamo of the Guardianship. Only in America, however, could the building of the administrative order proceed steadily, unhindered by restrictions, persecution, and the ravages of war.

'Abdu'l-Bahá had chosen America and given it primacy in the implementation of His Divine Plan.[10] It had developed " 'powers and capacities,' " He said, that would enable it to be the " 'first to build the Tabernacle of the Most Great Peace, and proclaim the oneness of mankind' " throughout the world.[11] As a result of His visit to North America in 1912, the light of Divine Revelation that had risen in the East was shining upon the West, even as the Báb had foretold. America was being prepared by the Hand of God to be "the cradle and stronghold of the Administrative Order of the Faith of Bahá'u'lláh," the land from which the Call of the Kingdom would be raised in all regions.[12] "*The American continent gives signs and evidences of very great advancement,*" 'Abdu'l-Bahá had said; "*Its future is even more promising. . . . It will lead all nations spiritually.*"[13]

An early milestone was the formulation of the Declaration of Trust and By-Laws of the National Spiritual Assembly of the Bahá'ís of the United States and Canada. Five years later a similar document for Local Spiritual Assemblies was formulated and adopted by the Spiritual Assembly of New York City. Both became patterns Bahá'í communities around the world would follow. These documents defined the character and purpose of the Bahá'í community, the method of elections, and the authority and functions of elected Assemblies. They set out the relationship of these bodies to each other, to the Guardian, and to The Universal House of Justice and provided a legal basis for incorporation and for the ownership of property. The national charters, Shoghi Effendi stated, would pave the way for the constitution "upon which the blest and sanctified edifice of the first International House of Justice" would one day "securely rest and flourish."[14]

TRIBULATION AND TRIUMPH

Sixteen years would elapse before the world mission outlined in the Tablets of the Divine Plan could begin. During this period the Faith remained mostly in the shadow of the world's attention, leaving the Bahá'í community free to proceed actively with the building of its administrative order. However, a number of attacks and persecutions occurred that brought the Faith to the attention of world leaders. 'Abdu'l-Bahá had warned that such attacks would come and grow more fierce in the future, initially from fanatical religious leaders who would fear the loss of their power and position. As the Faith grew, enfolding all races, classes, and religions, envious minds would be seized with jealousy and suspicion. Nevertheless, these attacks, borne steadfastly by the friends, would only cause the Faith to advance more swiftly and strongly.

Such an attack soon came in Baghdád. The House of Bahá'u'lláh, declared by Him to be a place of future pilgrimage, was seized by enemies in 1925. When all appeals through the religious courts of the land failed, the case was brought before the League of Nations. The Permanent Mandates Commission ruled in favor of the Bahá'í claim. 'Iráq, then under British Mandate, was pressed for action—but none came. Year after year the League's Commission expressed its concern.

Mountford Mills, an international lawyer and a member of the National Spiritual Assembly of the United States and Canada, acting on behalf of Shoghi Effendi, had several audiences with

King Feisal of 'Iráq and the king assured him 'Iráq would comply with the League's decision. Then a series of events, including the death of the 'Iráqí prime minister and of King Feisal himself, as well as 'Iráq's admission to the League in 1932, brought matters to a standstill. Bahá'u'lláh had foretold both the calamity and the eventual liberation of His House: "*Grieve not, O House of God, if the veil of thy sanctity be rent asunder. . . .*" "*In the fullness of time, the Lord shall, by the power of truth, exalt it in the eyes of all men.*"[15] Though outwardly a calamity, the Guardian declared, this event served to bring the Faith to the attention of governments and world leaders as nothing else had done since the birth of the Formative Age.

During the same period, the Bahá'ís of Egypt suffered grave injustices through rulings of the Muslim ecclesiastical court. They were declared heretics, denied the use of cemeteries, and harassed by many other legal difficulties. At this time the highest Muslim court ruled the Bahá'í Faith to be a new, independent religion, entirely outside the laws of Islám. This verdict was intended to bring humiliation and hardship upon the Bahá'ís of Egypt, which in many ways it did. But it also became, in the words of Shoghi Effendi, "the first Charter of the emancipation of the Cause of Bahá'u'lláh from the fetters of Islamic orthodoxy."[16]

Difficulties of a different nature arose for the believers in Turkistán (now under the Soviet regime), where a Bahá'í community had flourished since the days of Bahá'u'lláh. Bahá'í schools were already in operation in 1897, and the first House of Worship in the Bahá'í world had been built in 'Ishqábád in 1908. Believers there, as elsewhere in the world, were strictly obedient to their government and did not in any way mingle in political affairs. Nevertheless, the new regime imposed restrictions in 1928. Ten years later the civil authorities confiscated the Bahá'í Temple, closed the schools, and disbanded the Bahá'í community.

PERSIAN AND AMERICAN TIES

Persia, the cradle of the Faith, whose earth had been stained by the blood of the martyrs and of the blessed Báb Himself, is second only to the Holy Land in ties that bind together the hearts of the

Bahá'ís. Its leaders inflicted untold pain and hardship on the Promised One of God and banished Him from His homeland forever. Yet, of Persia's future Bahá'u'lláh has written: "*Let nothing grieve thee, O Land of Ṭá (Ṭihrán), for God hath chosen thee to be the source of the joy to all mankind. . . . The day is approaching when thy agitation will have been transmuted into peace and quiet calm.*"[17]

The fall of the Qájár dynasty and the coming of a new, more enlightened regime gave hope to the Bahá'ís that the longed-for day of "*peace and quiet calm*" was in some degree approaching. The Master had sent many Persian teachers to America, and the Persian Bahá'ís looked for the day when Bahá'ís from the West would come to their aid, as promised. In 1928 Shoghi Effendi asked Dr. Susan Moody, now seventy-seven years old, to return to Persia. She had earlier spent fifteen years in Ṭihrán and, assisted at various times by other believers, had played an important part in the founding of the Tarbíyat schools, established medical services for women, and aided the repressed women of that land to raise their status. She was highly honored by the Persian government. But persecution arose again and was at its height when she died in 1934. Schools that had served Bahá'ís and non-Bahá'ís alike were closed throughout Persia. Bahá'í centers were seized. Bahá'í literature was banned.

In the summer of 1932 Keith Ransom-Kehler, representing the National Spiritual Assembly of the United States and Canada, made a historic journey to Persia to appeal in person to the sháh. This followed many weeks of counsel from the Guardian in the Holy Land. Her first interview with the minister of the court promised an immediate removal of the ban on literature. But this did not take place, and shortly afterward the minister himself was removed from office. During the course of fifteen months Mrs. Ransom-Kehler made repeated appeals to the sháh. No acknowledgement came; no interview was granted. In addition to pouring out her mind and spirit on this mission, she traveled thousands of miles throughout Persia, meeting the Bahá'ís, teaching administration, encouraging Bahá'í women to take their rightful place in the work of the Faith. Long, heartbreaking months of striving and waiting, as well as ceaseless efforts to meet with Bahá'ís ex-

The Opening of the Formative Age 11

hausted her. She contracted smallpox in Iṣfahán and died within a few days, on October 23, 1933. She was buried near the graves of the King of Martyrs and the Beloved of Martyrs, heroic brothers sacrificed in the time of Bahá'u'lláh. The soil of Persia now received the remains of the "first and distinguished [American] martyr" and a Hand of the Cause of God from the West, Shoghi Effendi having elevated her to that rank at her passing.[18] She was one of those whom the Guardian later called "three heroines" of the Faith in America.[19] The others were Martha Root and May Maxwell.

THE FIRST TO ARISE

Although the Tablets of the Divine Plan would not be put into operation with an organized teaching plan until 1937, there were those who arose early to carry the Message around the world. Even before the revelation of the Tablets great services had been rendered by Lua Getsinger, who had gone to India at the Master's request and later died in Egypt in 1916; by Alma Knobloch in Germany and her sister Fanny in South Africa; and by many others elsewhere in the world.

Among the most notable responses made to the Tablets were the unique services of Martha Root in Latin America, Europe, and the Orient; of Hyde and Clara Dunn in Australia; and of Mrs. H. Emogene Hoagg and Marion Jack in Alaska.

Martha Root, who became the "star-servant" of Bahá'u'lláh,[20] was the first to arise in 1919, the very year the Tablets were read in New York City.* For twenty years she traveled the world as a journalist, spreading the Teachings, circling the globe four times. At all times she was in close touch with Shoghi Effendi and under his guidance. In Japan she assisted Agnes Alexander, who had already taken the Message there by 1914. Because of the Master's special emphasis on the future of China Martha visited that vast country four times. She enlisted in the Cause a Chinese professor,

---

*The Tablets of the Divine Plan, revealed during 1916-17, were not received until after the Armistice ending the First World War, when communication with the Holy Land was restored.

Dr. Y. S. Tsao, who immediately began translating Bahá'í literature into Chinese.

Dowager Queen Marie of Rumania, granddaughter of Queen Victoria, accepted the Faith through Martha and received her visits many times. The queen expressed deep appreciation of the Teachings publicly, as did many other world leaders, through Martha Root's efforts. Martha Root brought the Faith to Latin America as early as 1919, once crossing the Andes on a mule. The Bahá'ís of India and Burma welcomed her on three visits and gratefully utilized her services. She interviewed scores of their high dignitaries and spoke to packed university halls, often accompanied by Professor Pritam Singh, himself a tireless worker for the Cause in India. Australia and New Zealand were stirred to new levels of activity through her visits during which she secured unprecedented publicity. At the wish of the Guardian, she arranged for the translation and publication of Bahá'í literature in many languages, especially Dr. J. E. Esslemont's *Bahá'u'lláh and the New Era*.

Martha Root lies buried in Hawaii, halfway between East and West, where she fell, ill and exhausted, in the autumn of 1939. She was the "archetype of Bahá'í itinerant teachers," wrote Shoghi Effendi, "and the foremost Hand raised by Bahá'u'lláh since 'Abdu'l-Bahá's passing." He called her the "Leading Ambassadress of His Faith and Pride of Bahá'í teachers, whether men or women, in both the East and the West."[21]

Hyde and Clara Dunn, later named Hands of the Cause of God, arrived in Sydney, Australia, from America in 1920, to become its spiritual conquerors.[22] They took the Message of Bahá'u'lláh to New Zealand in 1922. Three years later the Bahá'í magazine *Herald of the South* began publication. An Assembly was raised in Melbourne in 1923 through the efforts of the Dunns. They welcomed the visits of Martha Root, and of Keith Ransom-Kehler on her Far Eastern journey in 1930. On Keith's visit to New Zealand the Message was taken to several Maori villages. A National Assembly for Australia and New Zealand was formed in 1934, and the first summer school was established at Yerrinbool, Australia, in 1938.

Marion Jack of Canada, an early pioneer to Alaska, went to Europe in the 1920s. By 1930 she had found her true goal,

The Opening of the Formative Age 13

Bulgaria, and stayed there for the remaining twenty-four years of her life. Her desire to remain at this post persuaded the Guardian to let her stay through the danger and hardship of the Second World War. At one time she was ably assisted by George Adam Benke, a native of Russia, who had been taught the Faith by Alma Knobloch in Germany and who, laying down his life in his arduous pioneer post, became the first European Bahá'í martyr. Marion Jack was an "immortal heroine," Shoghi Effendi cabled at the time of her death in 1954, a "shining example pioneers present future generations East West."[23]

Another who responded early to the Tablets was Leonora Holsapple Armstrong, the " 'mother of the Bahá'ís of Brazil.' "[24] She was honored there in February 1971 for fifty years of constant service to the Cause and soon thereafter was appointed to the Continental Board of Counselors in South America. Johanna Schubarth returned from America to her native Norway in 1927 to nurse her mother and at the Guardian's request remained until her own death in 1952. He named her the " 'mother of the Norwegian Bahá'í Community,' " the " 'founder of the Faith in that country.' "[25]

These are among the immortal heroes and heroines of the Faith whose hearts responded to the call of the Master and who, with the encouragement of the beloved Guardian, served steadfastly to the end of their days. Their self-sacrifice was to become an example and an inspiration for all the pioneers who would arise in years to come, when the great teaching campaigns were launched by Shoghi Effendi.

BETWEEN WARS IN EUROPE

The old Europe of the nineteenth century, whose rulers had been called to account by Bahá'u'lláh, was shattered by the Great War of 1914-18. Out of the chaos a League of Nations was born. One of its first setbacks was its rejection by the government of the United States whose president, Woodrow Wilson, the Guardian wrote in *God Passes By*, "imbibing some of the principles so clearly enunciated by Him ['Abdu'l-Bahá] in His discourses . . . incorporated them in a Peace Program which stands out as the

… boldest and noblest proposal yet made for the well-being and security of mankind.'' [26] The Master had already observed in His Tablet to the Central Organization for a Durable Peace, The Hague, dated December 17, 1919, that the League suffered from grave limitations. [27] The principles given by Bahá'u'lláh to ensure peace were sadly lacking in the vision of most if its framers. There was no power to enforce its sanctions. In the end the short-sightedness of the nations prevailed. Nonetheless, in the years following the First World War, which also marked the beginning of the Formative Age of the Faith, the League of Nations, seated in Geneva, was a source of hope and idealism to many peace-loving people.

Geneva became the seat of many world movements and peace organizations. An International Bahá'í Bureau was founded there in 1925 through the efforts of Mme Jeanne Stannards and under the guidance of the Guardian. The story of the development of the Bureau and the services contributed to it by Mrs. H. Emogene Hoagg, Miss Julia Culver, Mrs. Helen Bishop, Lady Blomfield, and others from various countries, is told elsewhere. [28] Its international status was soon recognized by the Federation of International Movements and later by the League itself. Lectures on peace and other matters of international interest were given there by Bahá'ís and others. Esperanto congresses were convened, organized by Martha Root and Lidia Zamenhof, daughter of the founder of this auxiliary language, whom Martha had attracted to the Faith. Visitors came to the Center from many countries. One of these was George Townshend, at that time Canon of St. Patrick's Cathedral, Dublin, and Archdeacon of Clonfert—positions he later renounced to devote his entire effort to the service of Bahá'u'lláh. Following a visit to the Bureau in October 1929 he wrote that the spirit there echoed that of Haifa.

The Bahá'í Messenger, partially supported by donations from Shoghi Effendi, was published by the Bureau in English, French, and German. Although the Bureau had no administrative authority in the Faith, it linked, in various ways, the work of Bahá'ís in many countries. One of its most useful services was the translation and publication of literature. This work advanced greatly through

The Opening of the Formative Age 15

the efforts of Anne Lynch, a Bahá'í of Russian origin, fluent in five other languages. The Bureau was a special source of encouragement to Bahá'ís during and after World War II, until 1957 when it closed.

The tragedy of World War II had its opening scene in Germany, a land that only a few decades earlier had seen " 'the banks of the Rhine . . . covered with gore,' " as Bahá'u'lláh had warned.[29] In 1923 the Bahá'ís had formed a National Assembly of Germany and Austria. The first summer school of Europe began in Esslingen, Germany, a site once blessed by the Master's footsteps. Among its early teachers were Dr. Adelbert Mühlschlegel and Dr. Hermann Grossmann, both later to be named Hands of the Cause of God. Then the dark shadows cast by the Nazi regime, which seized power in the spring of 1933, began to reach across the land. Germany withdrew from the League of Nations. The Esslingen school, which had seen such a bright array of international visitors, was closed in 1936 by an order of the government. That summer the school had reached a high point. May Maxwell, a distinguished disciple of the Master, was present with her daughter Mary, who had been teaching for many months in Germany.* In June 1937 the German National Assembly was forced to dissolve, and all Bahá'í activities were forbidden.

Even before the turn of the century France had been illumined by the teaching work of May Maxwell. She had been deeply attracted to the Cause through Lua Getsinger, one of the first American believers, whom Shoghi Effendi described as the "mother teacher of the West."[30] Soon after this, in 1898, May journeyed from Paris to 'Akká with Lua in the first party of Western pilgrims to visit 'Abdu'l-Bahá. May returned to Paris aflame with the Teachings to attract many who would become brilliant teachers of the Faith. Among these were Edith McKay (de Bons), the first believer in France; Edith Sanderson; Marion Jack; Thomas Breakwell, the first English Bahá'í; Laura Barney, the

---

*The following March a cable from the Holy Land announced the "honor conferred upon handmaid of Bahá'u'lláh Rúḥíyyih Khánum Miss Mary Maxwell" through her marriage to the Guardian.—"Mother of the Guardian Announces His Marriage," Bahá'í News, no. 107 (Apr. 1937), p. 1.

interlocutor of *Some Answered Questions*; and Hippolyte Dreyfus, the first native-born French believer.

Hippolyte Dreyfus wrote many books on the Faith and translated Bahá'í Writings into French. At one time he presented the Bahá'í Teachings at a meeting in Lyons presided over by the celebrated French statesman Édouard Herriott. Until his death in 1928 Dreyfus assisted Shoghi Effendi in a number of vital international matters. France distinguished itself in the early formative years by holding an annual conference in Paris for all Bahá'í university students in Europe.

Most countries of Western Europe had some resident believers during this period. Louisa Gregory, wife of Louis Gregory (who, at his passing, was the first Negro to be named a Hand of the Cause of God), went to the Balkans in 1928 and helped form the first Bahá'í group in Belgrade. Literature was available in most European languages. By 1937 *Bahá'u'lláh and the New Era* had been published in thirty-five languages.

This book, first published in England in 1923, was to become one of the most potent teaching tools of the Cause. A year after it appeared, the author, Dr. John E. Esslemont, a physician of Scottish descent, went to Haifa to assist the Guardian. He served there for a year until his untimely death and lies buried at the foot of Carmel. He was posthumously appointed a Hand of the Cause of God. His book, Shoghi Effendi said, would "alone, inspire generations yet unborn to tread the path of truth," a prediction that has already been abundantly fulfilled.[31]

England had been the scene of the Master's first public address in the West. At the City Temple, London, on September 10, 1911, He declared that the hour of unity of the sons of men had arrived. These words were echoed in the autumn of 1924 before a large gathering at the Conference of Some Living Religions Within the British Empire when Mountford Mills read a paper that Horace Holley—later to become a Hand of the Cause of God—had written for this noted event at Shoghi Effendi's request.

A World Congress of Faiths, broader in scope than the 1924 conference, was held in London in 1936. Sir Herbert Samuel, later Viscount Samuel of Carmel, paid a glowing tribute to the Bahá'í

The Opening of the Formative Age

Faith: "Other faiths and creeds have to consider . . . in what way they can contribute to the idea of world fellowship. But the Bahá'í faith exists almost for the sole purpose of contributing to the fellowship and the unity of mankind."[32] The Venerable Archdeacon George Townshend of Ireland prepared a Bahá'í paper for the conference. His brilliant book *The Promise of All Ages* had already been published, a harbinger of many more to come that would so greatly enrich the literature of the Faith.[33] The year 1936 was a significant one for the Bahá'ís of the British Isles: The first summer school was held in August at Matlock Bath; and the British *Bahá'í Journal*, which was to receive high praise from Shoghi Effendi, began publication. In 1932 the Bahá'í Publishing Trust was formed; Shoghi Effendi called upon the British believers to build and develop it with the same dedication that the American friends had given to the building of the Temple in America.

War clouds were now spreading swiftly over Europe and the world. Mussolini's attack on Ethiopia in 1935, the civil war that erupted in Spain in 1936, and the haste of nations to build up arms were signs of the coming convulsion and chaos.

THE FAR EAST

The Far East was not spared. Conflict between Japan and China broke out on Chinese soil in 1937. Martha Root herself narrowly escaped from Shanghai, which was under Japanese bombardment. She went to India to spend fifteen months. The National Spiritual Assembly of India wrote of her visit that it was " 'The most outstanding feature in the year' "; she " 'opened the whole of India for us.' "[34]

India had been one of the first countries to receive the Faith. The Báb Himself had sent an Indian, one of His eighteen Letters of the Living, to India. In 1875 Bahá'u'lláh sent India one of its first teachers, Jamál Effendi, who with Siyyid Muṣṭafá Rúmí, one of the first believers in India, opened Burma shortly thereafter. Siyyid-i-Rúmí remained in Burma the rest of his life, bringing an entire village, Daidanaw, into the Faith. In 1899 he took to the Holy Land the marble casket that the Bahá'ís of Mandalay had made to hold the precious remains of the Báb. He translated many passages from the Writings into Burmese and founded numerous Bahá'í centers.

The vast Indian subcontinent, with its many languages, presented challenges far greater than those confronting many other communities. By the 1930s *Bahá'u'lláh and the New Era* was already published in Urdu, Hindi, Bengali, Sindhi, Gujarati, and Burmese. India was one of the first communities to proclaim the Faith widely to large audiences. Thousands heard of the Teachings in the early formative years through talks at universities, from the platforms of religious and philosophical societies, and through the participation of Bahá'ís in various cultural events. Bahá'í women began early to take part in administrative work. One of the first women of the East to speak on a public platform was a Bahá'í, Mrs. Shirin Fozdar. She represented women of both India and Persia at an All-Asian Women's Conference in Lahore in 1931. A Bahá'í summer school was first opened in 1938 in Simla, in the foothills of the Himalaya mountains. One of the first Bahá'ís of Hindu background, Narayenrao Vakil, attracted many believers from the Hindu community and served as chairman of the National Assembly for over twenty years. Professor Pritam Singh occupies a unique position in the history of the Bahá'í Faith in India. He was the first member of the Sikh community of India to accept Bahá'u'lláh and devoted his entire life, until his passing in 1959, to the promotion of the Bahá'í Faith.

THE PASSING OF THE GREATEST HOLY LEAF

For many years Bahá'í pilgrims had been privileged to enter the presence of 'Abdu'l-Bahá's *"well-beloved, deeply spiritual sister."*[35] They had shared, in the words of the Guardian, her "extreme sociability which made her accessible to all; a generosity, a love . . . that reflected so clearly the attributes of 'Abdu'l-Bahá's character; . . . a quiet and unassuming disposition that served to enhance a thousandfold the prestige of her exalted rank."[36] That rank, bestowed by Bahá'u'lláh, was a "*'station such as none other woman hath surpassed.'*"[37]

The Opening of the Formative Age 19

Bahíyyih Khánum shared the trials and ordeals of her Father, her beautiful, noble mother, Navváb, and her two brothers, from the early days of terror in Ṭihrán to the prison confinement in 'Akká. She was in that prison when her youngest brother, Mírzá Midhí, the Purest Branch, fell to his death from the roof. She lived for the purpose of serving Bahá'u'lláh and His Cause. When He ascended, she remained firmly with 'Abdu'l-Bahá against the "almost entire company of his faithless relatives."[38] The affairs of the Cause in the Holy Land were placed in her care when the Master made His western journeys.

It was Bahíyyih Khánum who cabled the news of the Master's passing and the appointment of Shoghi Effendi as Guardian to the Bahá'í world. She stood at the side of the young Guardian with a compassionate love and understanding, coupled with iron steadfastness in the Covenant, that made her a source of comfort and a tower of strength to Shoghi Effendi.

Named "Bahá'íyyih," she was better known as "Bahíyyih." The honorific "The Most Exalted Leaf," sometimes translated as "The Greatest Holy Leaf," which Bahá'u'lláh had conferred upon her blessed mother, Navváb, was bestowed upon Bahíyyih Khánum by her father after the passing of Navváb.

When Bahíyyih Khánum died in July 1932, Shoghi Effendi built a beautiful marble monument over her resting place on the side of Mount Carmel. He likened its design to the administrative order—its circular steps symbolizing the Local Spiritual Assemblies, its pillars the National Assemblies, its crowning dome The Universal House of Justice. She was "the last survivor of a glorious and heroic age," the Guardian wrote, and her death drew to a close the "most moving chapter of Bahá'í history."[39] She had lived to witness the first eleven years of the Formative Age and the steady development of the Administrative Order under the guidance of Shoghi Effendi. Seven years after her passing, Shoghi Effendi brought the sacred remains of her mother, Navváb, and of the Purest Branch, to rest beside her. This act, he stated, further reinforced the spiritual potencies of that sacred spot and released forces that would hasten the coming of the World Order of Bahá'u'lláh.[40]

THE MOTHER TEMPLE OF THE WEST

In the twilight years of the Greatest Holy Leaf, Shoghi Effendi had written to the believers in North America urging them to proceed with the building of the Bahá'í Temple, news of its progress being the "one remaining solace in her swiftly ebbing life."[41] Her longing and hope for this great Mother Temple of the West stemmed from the Master's words foretelling its glorious future in teaching the Faith.[42] The ground had been hallowed by His footsteps in 1912, but work had proceeded slowly during the first twenty years. Models of the Temple displayed in New York and Chicago art galleries drew the keen interest and admiration of many journalists and architects, including the president of the Architectural League. They called it a " ' "new creation," ' " a " 'Temple of Peace,' " the " 'temple of light.' "[43] Articles in journals published as far apart as New York and Tokyo described its features and explained its symbology.

Many nationalities and races had been present when the Master dedicated the Temple site in Wilmette, and contributions toward its construction came from all over the world. Corinne True, later named a Hand of the Cause of God, who had been honored by receiving the Master in her home in Chicago, served as the financial secretary, encouraging Bahá'ís in this vast undertaking that the Master had said was " 'the *most important of all things.*' "[44]

For eight years the circular basement, resting on steel caissons sunk 122 feet to bedrock, served as a meeting place, but the exterior was unsightly. In spite of the great economic depression that gripped the nation and the world, Bahá'ís pressed forward in 1930 to erect the superstructure. The architect, Louis Bourgeois, a French Canadian Bahá'í, died that same year. The casting of the beautiful, lacelike forms for the exterior began in 1932. A model shown at the Chicago Century of Progress Exposition in 1933 brought the Bahá'í Faith to the attention of thousands of people. When the first Seven Year Plan was launched in America in 1937, one of its chief goals was the completion of the Temple exterior by May 1944 to mark the end of the first century of the Faith.

AMERICA BEFORE THE FIRST SEVEN YEAR PLAN

EARLY PROCLAMATION AND TEACHING EFFORTS. Prior to the opening of the first Seven Year Plan in 1937, there were no organized teaching plans with specific goals. Nevertheless, many Bahá'ís arose to teach throughout North America, Europe, Latin America, Asia, and the Pacific Islands. The Faith had been proclaimed at expositions and conferences on peace and world affairs in the United States—echoes of its first mention in America in 1893 at the Columbian Exposition in Chicago. At that time religious leaders from all over the world, assembled at a World Parliament of Religions, had heard the name of Bahá'u'lláh read from a paper prepared by a Christian missionary who described Bahá'u'lláh's words as "noble, . . . Christ-like" and quoted His famed statement to Professor E. G. Browne of Cambridge University " 'That all nations should become one in faith and all men as brothers.' "[45]

Nineteen years later the Master Himself declared in San Francisco: *"The age has dawned when human fellowship will become a reality. . . . all mankind shall dwell in peace and security beneath the shelter of the . . . one living God."* [46] In 1925 this theme was publicly proclaimed again in San Francisco through a World Unity Conference which the Bahá'ís organized and in which outstanding civic leaders participated.

The first Bahá'í Race Amity Conference was convened in 1921 in Washington, D.C., at the Master's request, largely through the efforts of Mrs. Agnes Parsons. It became the "mother" of a series of similar events which eventually grew into the annual Race Unity Day observed by hundreds of Bahá'í communities. Shoghi Effendi was quick to praise this effort but also urged Bahá'ís to be "living witnesses" to race unity, after the example set by the Master in America.[47] Louis Gregory, who had participated in the Conference, was the first Bahá'í to make regular circuits to speak on the Faith at Negro colleges in the South. He and Willard McKay became the first racially integrated teaching team in the South, in 1931—a courageous undertaking at that time. Dorothy Baker, later named a Hand of the Cause of God, followed some few years after, fearlessly giving the Teachings in more than ninety southern colleges, both for whites and blacks.

The Souvenir of 'Abdu'l-Bahá at West Englewood, New Jersey, became an annual event in memory of the Feast given there by 'Abdu'l-Bahá in 1912. The property itself was donated in 1935 by Roy Wilhelm, who was named a Hand of the Cause of God at his passing.

The first summer school in the United States began at Green Acre in Eliot, Maine, on America's eastern shore. The Faith had been represented there, along with many other religious and cultural movements, before the Master's visit to it in 1912. This open forum of a liberal nature had been conceived in 1892 by Sarah Farmer, daughter of a well-known American inventor.* Sarah became attracted to the Faith and visited the Master in 'Akká in 1900. Thereafter Green Acre steadily developed a greater emphasis on the Teachings of Bahá'u'lláh. It became Bahá'í property in 1929. A Pacific school was opened at Geyserville, California, in 1927, at the ranch home of John and Louisa Bosch, early believers who deeded it to the Bahá'í Trustees in 1935. Louhelen Bahá'í School, located in the heart of America near Davison, Michigan, held its first sessions in 1931 through the efforts of Mr. and Mrs. Lou Eggleston.

PUBLICATION BEFORE THE FIRST SEVEN YEAR PLAN. When *The Dawn-Breakers* was first published in the United States in 1932, Shoghi Effendi said it should become an "unchallengeable textbook" in the summer schools, giving the Bahá'ís of the West an understanding of the spirit that moved the believers of the early Heroic Age.[48] Shoghi Effendi himself compiled, edited, and translated this monumental work, even directing details of its design. During the sixteen years of preparation before the first plan was launched, literature in English was greatly expanded through the publication of many outstanding texts, particularly Shoghi Effendi's translations of the Writings of Bahá'u'lláh. In addition to various Prayers and Tablets, he translated the following works:

---

*Among notable figures associated with these programs were John Greenleaf Whittier, noted American poet; Booker T. Washington; and, at a later time, Mírzá Abu'l-Faḍl, well-known Persian scholar and learned apologist of the Bahá'í Faith.

The *Kitáb-i-Íqán* (The Book of Certitude), *The Hidden Words of Bahá'u'lláh* (published earlier in England in his own translation), *Gleanings from the Writings of Bahá'u'lláh*, and *Prayers and Meditations by Bahá'u'lláh*.[49] With *Some Answered Questions, Paris Talks,* and *Bahá'u'lláh and the New Era*, all first published in England, various compilations of the Master's talks in the West, and an increasingly diversified list of books and pamphlets written by Bahá'ís, the believers of this time had a greatly enriched treasury of the scriptural, interpretive, and expository literature of their Faith in the English language.[50]

Magazine publication in America began in March 1910 with *Star of the West* (called *Bahá'í News* its first year and *The Bahá'í Magazine* in its concluding years, until it was discontinued in March 1935). At this time *World Order* was born, a new magazine that was the product of a union of *Bahá'í Magazine* and *World Unity* magazine. The latter publication had been published by a group of individuals that included Bahá'ís and others, with the aim of promoting the ideals of world unity among the general public. Horace Holley was the managing editor, and a number of world figures served as contributing editors, among them Havelock Ellis, Auguste Forel, Kahlil Gibran, David Starr Jordan, Harry Allen Overstreet, and Frank Lloyd Wright. Shoghi Effendi highly approved combining the two magazines under the name *World Order*, to function under the National Spiritual Assembly and give a broader, more influential medium for the public expression of the Bahá'í Teachings. The first issue of *World Order* magazine was published in April 1935.[51]

Bahá'í News (called *Bahá'í News Letter* in the beginning) was first published in December 1924 and continued thereafter as a monthly journal of news and information for Bahá'ís only.

A unique publishing endeavor began in 1926 with the first volume of *The Bahá'í World*, initially called *The Bahá'í Year Book*. This enterprise was based upon a suggestion from Horace Holley, who labored devotedly as secretary of the American National Assembly to develop the Administrative Order under the Guardian's guidance. Publishing *The Bahá'í World* received Shoghi Effendi's wholehearted support—he personally selected and arranged the contents of twelve consecutive volumes in his lifetime, all of which were published in the United States under the aegis of the National Spiritual Assembly. The content of these volumes, consisting of a review of international events and documentary material relating to the progress of the Faith, was, beginning with Volume II, compiled by an international board of editors under the supervision of Shoghi Effendi.[52] As succeeding editions were published, over the years, thousands of copies were presented to public and university libraries throughout the world and to local, national, and international leaders.

Many believers of the Master's time had been attracted to the Cause by the spirit of the "return." 'Abdu'l-Bahá's fatherly love and noble example, movingly recounted in Howard Colby Ives' book *Portals to Freedom*, did more to motivate them to carry out His admonitions than any concept of laying the foundation of a divinely ordained social pattern that they, as yet, could but dimly perceive.[53] It was not only the Guardian's great task to lay the foundation of the Administrative Order as the base for launching the Divine Plan but also to educate the Bahá'ís in the meaning of the World Order of Bahá'u'lláh.

Between 1929 and 1936 Shoghi Effendi wrote a series of seven major letters later published in one volume as *The World Order of Bahá'u'lláh*.[54] These letters developed the theme of a divine economy enshrined in Bahá'u'lláh's Revelation. They presented a world approaching the edge of catastrophe, its religious and political institutions unable to stop the drift, and explained the society-building power of the new Revelation. Two forces were at work, Shoghi Effendi declared, the crumbling of an old order and the building of a new one. The work of Bahá'ís in spreading the Faith, with its spirit of unity reflected in its own administrative order, was at the heart of the integrating process. The Lesser Peace, offered by Bahá'u'lláh to a world that had refused His Most Great Peace, would be a political union of the nations, though a spiritually hungry humanity would not find contentment until it turned wholeheartedly to the Teachings of Bahá'u'lláh. North America's role in achieving that Most Great Peace was analyzed in one letter, and the believers were admonished not to relinquish their God-

The Opening of the Formative Age 25

given responsibility and primacy. *The Dispensation of Bahá'u'-lláh*, published in 1934, cast a brilliant light upon the Faith itself, the stations of its Central Figures, its links with past and future Dispensations, and the manner in which the creative energies released through Bahá'u'lláh's laws worked through His Administrative Order.[55] The last message of the series, published in 1936, entitled *The Unfoldment of World Civilization*, gave a broad view of the titanic, spiritual upheaval taking place throughout the world in all areas of human life, as society struggled toward the coming of age of the entire human race.[56] This analysis of the processes released by Bahá'u'lláh, coupled with an illuminating glimpse of its consummation in a future Golden Age, immensely expanded the believers' understanding of their sacred, glorious task.

THE PROMULGATION OF THE DIVINE PLAN

"A new hour has struck," Shoghi Effendi announced to the North American believers in 1935.[57] The next year, amidst the "deepening gloom" of the world, he wrote that the time was drawing near for the Message of Bahá'u'lláh to be carried to the "countless multitudes that hunger for its teachings."[58] Late in that same year he further exhorted the American believers: "The promulgation of the Divine Plan . . . is the key which Providence has placed in the hands of the American believers whereby to unlock the doors leading them to fulfil their unimaginably glorious Destiny."[59]

THE FIRST SEVEN YEAR PLAN (1937-1944). So critical was this hour in history that the Guardian asked the delegates to the Annual Convention of the United States and Canada in 1937 to prolong their sessions and deliberate on the tasks assigned to them in the Seven Year Plan. The chief objectives of this Plan were: (1) the completion of the exterior of the Temple in Wilmette; (2) the formation of a Spiritual Assembly in each state and province of North America and in Alaska; and (3) the establishment of a center in each republic of Latin America and the Caribbean.

This Seven Year Plan, initiated by the Guardian, constituted the first organized response of the American believers to the mandate given to them in 'Abdu'l-Bahá's Divine Plan and was the first systematic teaching plan in the Bahá'í world. As other National Spiritual Assemblies were formed and gained in strength, they developed active campaigns and were given similar plans, largely aimed, at this time, toward their own internal expansion. At a later time all the National Assemblies would become the "generals" of Bahá'u'lláh's "army of light," joining forces in the "most glorious Crusade ever launched in the course of Bahá'í history for the systematic propagation of the Cause of Bahá'u'lláh over the surface of the entire planet."[60]

Now a spiritual army began to take shape in America. Goals were mapped out, committees appointed, funds established, spiritual warriors moved into position. The first big exodus of pioneers began. "To try, to persevere, is to ensure ultimate and complete victory," exclaimed the Guardian.[61] An early prize was the formation in 1938 of the first Latin American Spiritual Assembly in Mexico City. The Guardian's heart was exhilarated by the "unbroken solidarity and unquenchable enthusiasm" that distinguished this new enterprise.[62]

On December 25, 1938, Shoghi Effendi dispatched a long letter that might be termed a permanent guide for every Bahá'í teacher and pioneer. Published as *The Advent of Divine Justice*, it referred again to North America's leading role in proclaiming Bahá'u'lláh's Teachings to the world—that continent now being the location of the "chief remaining citadel" of the Faith in a world that had become an "armed camp."[63] The resounding call was to arise and teach; its watchword, the conduct and character of each Bahá'í. The soldiers in the spiritual army of Bahá'u'lláh must stand out brightly against the darkness of the materialism and moral laxity of their culture and show complete freedom from every kind of prejudice. Both black and white must do their part to heal the wounds of the past. Teaching the Faith of Bahá'u'lláh must also include deepening in understanding of His Mission. The Guardian named an early target for the present Plan: planting the banner of the Faith in Panama, that meeting place of the Atlantic and Pacific Oceans, an area to which the Master had attached great importance in His Tablets.

In the spring of 1939 Shoghi Effendi warned of the imminent

The Opening of the Formative Age   27

eruption of war. It burst upon Europe in August of that year, a few weeks before the passing of Martha Root in Hawaii. Six months later May Maxwell, spiritual mother of the Faith in France and Canada, won her "'martyr's crown" in Argentina, laying down her life at this southern outpost of the Faith.[64] She was the last of America's "three heroines" whose dust now lay in far-off continents and islands.[65] The passing of these two handmaidens at this time assured the triumph of the new Plan, Shoghi Effendi wrote.[66]

A Bahá'í International School, which was created through the generosity of Loulie Mathews of the Inter-America Committee, opened in Colorado in 1940 especially to train pioneer teachers for the Latin American campaign. When the midpoint of the Plan arrived, three Assemblies and five groups had been established in Latin America, and literature was being published there. A news bulletin linked these new outposts, and Shoghi Effendi expressed a desire to correspond directly with each pioneer.

The war in Europe spread, threatening the Holy Land. In 1941 Shoghi Effendi wrote *The Promised Day Is Come*, giving the Bahá'ís a better understanding of this destructive chapter in human history. The "judgment of God" was upon the world, he wrote, preparing it for the Day foretold in the Holy Books of the past.[67] Secular and religious leaders had ignored the healing Message, and now they were powerless to avert calamity. In spite of the present turmoil the Guardian assured the Bahá'ís that they should "labor serenely, confidently and unremittingly" to lead humanity out of its misery.[68] The Japanese attack on Pearl Harbor in December 1941 catapulted the United States into the war, both in Europe and the Pacific. Although hardship and restrictions followed, the pioneers continued to leave for positions in Latin America and throughout North America.

The Temple exterior was completed early in 1943, and the first Alaskan Assembly was formed that year, in Anchorage. Shortwave programs were beamed to South America. Seven Assemblies were still needed in North America—and only a year remained in the Plan. A mighty effort was launched, using every type of proclamation and teaching facility at hand. When March of 1944 came, the last three Canadian Assemblies had been formed; it was the final seal of victory![69]

THE FIRST CENTENARY OF THE FAITH

War still raged in both hemispheres as Bahá'ís gathered in meetings around the world to celebrate the centenary of the Declaration of the Báb in <u>Sh</u>íráz on the eve of May 23, 1844. A century earlier He had called to the West to arise and proclaim the New Day. Now East and West joined in thanksgiving and praise to Him and to Bahá'u'lláh. In <u>Sh</u>íráz ninety delegates to the National Convention of Írán gathered to visit the upper room of the Báb's house where He had declared His Mission to Mullá Ḥusayn. In the Holy Land over 150 Bahá'ís heard the beloved Guardian chant in the Holy Shrines and later recount the thrilling progress of the Cause.

Some five hundred Egyptian Bahá'ís celebrated the occasion in their new Ḥaẓíratu'l-Quds—the dome having been completed only two hours earlier. 'Iráqí Bahá'ís scheduled six days of events with many visitors attending. In spite of harassment the believers of these lands had continued their heroic efforts in opening new areas, translating literature into Arabic, and encouraging the activity of youth.

The Australian Bahá'ís met in their newly acquired headquarters, now appropriately dedicated by "Mother" Dunn. The New Zealand Bahá'ís held a banquet meeting in Auckland. Bahá'ís there had recently witnessed the unique universality of the Faith through a talk given in an Anglican pulpit by an American Bahá'í serviceman of orthodox Jewish background.

The Mayor of Bombay opened India's observance. An intensive publicity campaign was mounted, resulting in the making of a news film. The Indian community had delighted the Guardian by launching its own Six Year Plan in 1938. At the Guardian's suggestion, its chief goal was sending pioneers to open new areas.

The valiant British Bahá'ís had not only survived the war but had managed to increase modestly their numbers despite severe hardship and restriction on travel. Their summer school had functioned every year of the war except 1940 when the threat of invasion was imminent. Now many cities arranged beautiful, informative exhibits—one of them attracting much attention in the heart of Westminster. Sir Ronald Storrs, first military Governor of

The Opening of the Formative Age

Jerusalem under the British Mandate, who had known and admired 'Abdu'l-Bahá for many decades, gave a warm tribute to the Faith at the London observance.

More than sixteen hundred Bahá'ís from North and South America gathered under the dome of the House of Worship in Wilmette to view the portrait of the Báb at its first showing in the West. It marked the final triumph of the Seven Year Plan. The Faith now reached from Alaska in the far North to Magallanes at the southern tip of South America. The beautiful exterior of the Mother Temple of the West, floodlit at night, gleamed like a heavenly jewel.

Shoghi Effendi issued a world survey of the Faith for the centenary.[70] The Cause had spread to seventy-eight countries, fifty-six of them sovereign states. Fifteen Spiritual Assemblies had been formed in Latin America, and there was a Bahá'í center in each republic. Literature was available in forty-nine languages. While the centenary celebrations were still in progress, the Guardian cabled a decision to proceed at an early date with the building of the Shrine of the Báb—the outer structure to enclose the one raised by 'Abdu'l-Bahá. It was designed by the distinguished Canadian architect William Sutherland Maxwell, the father of Amatu'l-Bahá Rúḥíyyih Khánum. He was later named a Hand of the Cause of God.

At a time when war was threatening the Holy Land, when the state of international communications was making the burden of guiding a world community even more difficult and while Covenant-breaking was spreading within his own family, Shoghi Effendi had the strength of mind and purpose to write his immortal book *God Passes By*.[71] One hundred years of the world's greatest religious drama are recorded in its pages. This chronicle of the forward march of the Cause of God, meeting crises of all kinds and emerging triumphant from tribulation, opened up a new vision to Bahá'ís, both of the past and of the future.

The Second Epoch of the Formative Age
(1944-1963)

THE AFTERMATH OF THE WAR

The Second World War ended officially on May 8, 1945, in Europe and on September 2 of that year in Japan. The foundations of the Cause in Europe and the Orient had been sorely tried but had held firm. The German Bahá'ís had suffered greatly but heroically. They had been brought to trial and placed in concentration camps; their literature and archives had been destroyed. Yet the Bahá'í community in this country, which Shoghi Effendi said was "destined to play an outstanding role in the spiritual revival" of Europe, rose quickly to its feet.[1] Marta Brauns-Forel of Karlsruhe, daughter of Dr. Auguste Forel, the famed Swiss scientist to whom the Master had addressed a Tablet, was one of many German believers who performed courageous services.[2] Another was Paul Gollmer of Stuttgart, who aided that community in obtaining an official permit to organize within a few months of the close of the war. Bahá'ís there and elsewhere in Germany were assisted in these efforts by Allied Bahá'í servicemen. The National Assembly of Germany and Austria was formed again in 1946.

In Japan American Bahá'í servicemen searched out the believers, among them the much-loved Fujita (Mr. Saichiro Fujita), who had come to the Holy Land in 1919 at the Master's invitation and had served there for nearly twenty years. The library of Agnes Alexander, with hundreds of precious copies in Japanese of Dr. Esslemont's book, was found intact in a ruined part of Tokyo. Four years were to pass before Tokyo would form its Spiritual Assembly in 1950.

The Indian subcontinent underwent fundamental changes during and after the war. The days of British rule ended. The land was divided by hatred and prejudice. New political boundaries were formed, and religious riots spread like wildfire; but the Bahá'í community forged ahead undivided. The Bahá'ís had increased their numbers during their Six Year Plan. Now they planned to triple their Assemblies by 1950 and to translate Dr. Esslemont's book into eighteen additional languages. New teaching zones were mapped out, and pioneer families—one each from Indian and Persian backgrounds—went forth to form the nuclei of new Bahá'í communities. The National Assembly of India and Burma summarized the essence of pioneering in these words: " 'The individual, the backbone of the whole scheme, will, in . . . pioneering, . . . develop the qualities of faith in God, in himself and in his fellowmen, the attributes of renunciation, of courage and audacity, of initiative and enterprise.' "[3]

The Burmese Bahá'ís had suffered severely during the war. One who died in the violence that swept the land was Siyyid Muṣṭafá Rúmí, at the age of ninety-nine. He was named a Hand of the Cause of God at his passing. An urgent goal for India was to assist the Burmese community to rise again.

THE FORMATION OF THE UNITED NATIONS

When the United Nations first convened in San Francisco on April 25, 1945, it was a significant event to Bahá'ís. Exactly thirty years earlier to the day, in San Francisco, Bahá'ís had taken part in an international peace conference that sent President Woodrow Wilson a message. Even more significant was the fact that 'Abdu'l-Bahá Himself had said in California in 1912, *"May the first flag of International Peace be upraised in this State."*[4] In 1945 the Bahá'ís seized their chance—presented by the opening of the United Nations—and arranged meetings, banquets, exhibits, radio programs, and press interviews. They presented a specially prepared brochure, *The Bahá'í Peace Program*, to thousands of delegates and observers and sent their own observers to the sessions.[5] Their efforts were so well noted that a leading Egyptian newspaper published an account of the Bahá'í activity and printed the contents of the brochure in full. The Honorable Sir Ramaswami Mudaliar, leader of the Indian delegation, was inspired to visit the Bahá'í Temple in Wilmette and later received a Bahá'í delegation in London. The following January the British Bahá'ís sent a letter and brochure to each United Nations delegate at the first meeting of the General Assembly in London. Encouraged and guided by Shoghi Effendi, the Bahá'ís expanded their interest and participation in the work of the United Nations. The National Spiritual Assembly of the Bahá'ís of the British Isles was one of the first members of the League of Nations Union in England, and this membership was later carried forward into the United Nations Association. The National Spiritual Assembly of the United States and Canada was first accredited by the United Nations as a nongovernmental organization in 1947; the Bahá'í International Community was accredited the following year. Bahá'í observers took part in United Nations nongovernmental conferences in many parts of the world. National Assemblies appointed committees to encourage local Bahá'í activity and support for the work of the United Nations. Carefully prepared documents based upon Bahá'í principles were formally submitted to this body, including *A Bahá'í Declaration of Human Obligations and Rights* and "A Bahá'í Statement on Rights of Women," both in 1947.[6] In 1955 delegates at the charter revision conference were presented by the Bahá'ís with *Proposals for Charter Revision*.[7]

In 1947 the United Nations Special Committee on Palestine asked Shoghi Effendi, as head of a Faith with its world center in Haifa, for a statement on the Bahá'í attitude toward Palestine and its future. The Guardian included with his reply a summary of the history and teachings of the Faith, later published and widely circulated as *The Faith of Bahá'u'lláh: A World Religion*.[8] In 1970, under the direction of The Universal House of Justice, the Bahá'í International Community was admitted as a nongovernmental organization to consultative status with the Economic and Social Council.

THE SECOND SEVEN YEAR PLAN (1946-1953)*

A GOD-GIVEN MANDATE. Less than a year had elapsed since the ending of the "greatest conflict that . . . [had] ever shaken the

---

*"The Second Seven Year Plan, intended to carry a stage further the mission conceived by 'Abdu'l-Bahá for the American Bahá'í Community, . . . must, as

human race" when Shoghi Effendi issued a call to the North American community to rise to "scale loftier heights of heroism."[9] Western Europe was the new spiritual frontier—that "war-torn, spiritually famished European continent, cradle of world-famed civilizations, twice-blest by 'Abdu'l-Bahá's visits, whose rulers Bahá'u'lláh specifically and collectively addressed."[10] A European Teaching Committee was formed, with an auxiliary office in Geneva. Ten goal countries were named: Portugal, Spain, Italy, Switzerland, Luxembourg, Belgium, Holland, Denmark, Norway, and Sweden—Finland would be added later. The first pioneers sailed within four months, "wholly dedicated souls, aglow with enthusiasm," but facing many physical hardships and spiritual challenges.[11] One of these, Dagmar Dole, was to be " 'the first to give her life for the Cause in the European project.' " " 'She died in "battle dress," ' " said the Guardian at the time of her passing in 1952; " 'it is wonderful to die in active service.' "[12]

Shoghi Effendi encouraged close collaboration between the British Publishing Trust and the German Publishing Committee to provide the needed literature quickly. By Riḍván 1948 there were new Bahá'ís in each goal city. The first European Teaching Conference held in Geneva in May 1948 was hailed by the Guardian as a landmark in the European campaign. Nearly a hundred Bahá'ís came from nineteen countries to share in a new fellowship and to plan further victories. A joyful cable from Shoghi Effendi urged them to continue to hold aloft "the torch of divine guidance."[13] Summer schools opened—the first in Switzerland in 1947. By March of 1952 progress was such as to move Shoghi Effendi to call for the formation of the Italo-Swiss National Spiritual Assembly at Riḍván 1953.

A few weeks after the inauguration of a new Seven Year Plan Shoghi Effendi issued a lengthy, cogent message published as "A God-Given Mandate."[14] It presented a panoramic view of the evolution of the Divine Plan from the birth of the Faith "in darkest

---

it operates in three continents, be productive of results outshining any as yet achieved since the Divine Plan itself was set in motion. . . ."—Shoghi Effendi, *Citadel of Faith: Messages to America, 1947-1957* (Wilmette, Ill.: Bahá'í Publishing Trust, 1965), pp. 6-7.

Persia" to that "ultimate redemption of all mankind." Again the Guardian stressed the significance of the Master's visits to the West, particularly His call to America to proclaim the " '*advent of the Kingdom of the Lord of Hosts* . . . *in all the five continents of the globe.*' "[15] The present stage of the Divine Plan would end at the hundredth anniversary of the " 'Year Nine' " that had marked the birth of Bahá'u'lláh's Mission in the Síyáh-Chál. Shoghi Effendi named it "Holy Year" to be observed in 1952-53.[16] A further projection in the evolution of the Divine Plan, he wrote, would be marked by the worldwide celebration of the "Most Great Festival," the "greatest of all Jubilees," related to the 1,335 days mentioned in the Book of Daniel.[17] This Great Festival was to be observed at Riḍván 1963. "A God-Given Mandate" was not only an appeal and a stirring challenge to the believers; it was also an assurance of victory to all who would arise to assume their God-given role.

Shoghi Effendi named other objectives of this plan: consolidation and expansion of the Faith throughout the Americas; completion of the House of Worship in Wilmette and landscaping of the grounds; the formation of National Spiritual Assemblies in Canada, in Central America, and in South America.

TEN NATIONAL PLANS CIRCLE THE WORLD

The first of the new pillars for The Universal House of Justice was raised in Canada where delegates met in April 1948 in the Maxwell home, which had been hallowed by the Master's presence in 1912.[18] Under the Guardian's direction the National Assembly of Canada initiated a Five Year Plan resulting in the establishment of thirty Local Assemblies from coast to coast, the opening of a hundred centers including ones in Greenland and Newfoundland, the enrollment of Eskimo and Indian believers, and the purchase of a Ḥaẓíratu'l-Quds in Toronto. In their second year the Canadian National Spiritual Assembly secured, through an Act of Parliament, incorporation by Royal Charter, which the Guardian termed unique in the history of the Bahá'í world and the strongest incorporation legally.

A sense of commitment intensified among Latin American

Bahá'ís as they assumed increasing responsibilities for the formation of their own National Spiritual Assemblies. Regional committees took shape in 1946, new Assemblies and groups were formed, and the number of believers doubled in a single year. Summer schools were organized in Argentina, Chile, and Mexico. Teaching conferences were convened in Buenos Aires and in Panama City, each to become the seat of a future National Assembly. In 1947 Shoghi Effendi addressed them in his long message to America, published as *The Challenging Requirements of the Present Hour*, as "co-workers and associates" in carrying out the Divine Plan.[19] When the two Latin American National Spiritual Assemblies were elected in Central America and South America at Riḍván 1951, he assigned them a threefold responsibility: consolidation of the administrative structure, intensifying the teaching work, and deepening the believers. Under this plan a Bahá'í Cultural Institute was established in the heart of the Indian country in Chichicastenango, Guatemala, and a Bahá'í school was held at "Karbilá" near Tegucigalpa, Honduras. Lifting their sights above their own horizons, Shoghi Efendi indicated to these two fledgling communities the combined efforts they would soon be called upon to make, with their sister communities in Australasia and the Indian subcontinent, toward the "Spiritual conquest of the multitudinous islands of the South Pacific Ocean."[20]

Australia and New Zealand far exceeded the original goals of the Six Year Plan on which they had spontaneously embarked in 1947, bringing their total number of Assemblies to seventeen and groups to forty. This plan, Shoghi Effendi said, would pave the way for that "mighty Crusade" whereby they would carry the Faith to the far-flung Pacific territories.[21] He attested "the vitality of the faith of the believers" in Australia, exemplified by the number of pioneers who went to virgin territories and by their purchase of a Temple site in Sydney.

India, Pakistan, and Burma also spontaneously adopted a Nineteen Month Plan, their third consecutive one since the systematic prosecution of 'Abdu'l-Bahá's Divine Plan had begun in 1937. It too was a "prelude to the mighty and historic Crusade" to be launched in the future.[22] Additional translations were published, and the following countries opened: Thailand, Malaya (with an

The Second Epoch of the Formative Age 37

Assembly in Singapore), Indonesia, Sarawak (with an Assembly in Kuching), Zanzibar, Madagascar, and Nepal. Eight Assemblies were formed on the home front. The New Era School in Panchgani was moved to larger premises, and progress was made toward its official recognition.

In 1944 the Bahá'ís of the British Isles began prosecution of a Six Year Plan under which they trebled the size of their community and established Spiritual Assemblies in nineteen cities. It was, in the Guardian's words, "one of the most significant undertakings embarked upon by the members of the Bahá'í National Assemblies during the opening years of the second Bahá'í Century."[23] Moreover, it was the harbinger of an even more remarkable achievement. During this period a wide proclamation of the Faith was effected through the publication of a statement by George Townshend in which he explained his reasons for resigning his orders and church offices. Entitled *The Old Churches and the New World-Faith*, it was sent to more than ten thousand religious and other leaders of public opinion.[24]

Still emerging from the war's devastation, the Bahá'ís of Germany and Austria nevertheless doubled their numbers by 1947. With his wisdom and compassion Shoghi Effendi guided them through this critical period of political and social unrest and in 1948 encouraged them to adopt a Five Year Plan. Because all literature had been destroyed, the publication of major Bahá'í books became a prime goal. A new Ḥaẓíratu'l-Quds was constructed in Frankfurt-am-Main; fourteen new communitites were raised and Spiritual Assemblies formed in nine of them. Esslingen Bahá'í School opened after a suspension of ten years.

Persia adopted a Forty-Five Month Plan in 1946. In addition to expansion of the national community, the goals included sending pioneers to India and 'Iráq an forming Assemblies in Afghanistan, in Arabia, and in the Persian Gulf. In the course of the Plan effective steps were taken to encourage Bahá'í women and to assist them in taking an active part in the affairs of the community. Shoghi Effendi paid tribute to the "glorious and continuing efforts rendered by the beloved Bahá'í sisters" of a land that had given Ṭáhirih to the world.[25]

Women were elected for the first time to Spiritual Assemblies in

Egypt in the course of that country's Five Year Plan, which began in May 1948. The Faith expanded in both Egypt and Sudan; centers were opened in Eritrea, Algeria, and Libya; and an Assembly was formed in Tunis in April 1953. Negotiations also began for the purchase of the House of Bahá'u'lláh in Istanbul (Constantinople), a project brought to conclusion in 1954.

'Iráq, whose Bahá'í community often shared the repression known to its sister communities in Persia and Egypt, is also a hallowed land to Bahá'ís. It had known the footsteps of Bahá'u'lláh during the first ten years of His exile and was the scene of His momentous Declaration in the Garden of Riḍván in Baghdád. During the years leading up to the Holy Year, the believers' devotion manifested itself in a plan during which they increased the number of centers, translated and published many additional titles in Arabic, and completed the construction of a national headquarters which included a spacious hall seating five hundred.

The midpoint of the second Seven Year Plan saw a financial crisis in the United States Bahá'í community. Costs for completing the Temple in Wilmette had risen greatly, and the expenses of two continental campaigns (Europe and Latin America) were formidable. Shoghi Effendi called for a period of austerity wherein certain activities would be temporarily suspended, a period later extended to the entire Bahá'í world. But the Divine Plan continued to go forward. When the Centenary of the Báb's martyrdom was observed on July 9, 1950, and the beautiful arcade and parapet of the Shrine were raised, the Guardian felt able to proceed with the completion of this "Queen of Carmel."[26] He released a new world survey to 1950. The Faith had reached a hundred countries—a gain of twenty-two in six years!

THE AFRICAN CAMPAIGN

Three years remained for the Bahá'í world to win its goals. Then Bahá'ís learned that plans aimed at the stars could aim even higher under the guiding hand of their Guardian. A new campaign was announced—Africa! Britain would spearhead and coordinate this challenging undertaking that called for the combined efforts of the

Bahá'ís of the British Isles, Egypt, India, Persia, and the United States. The British Bahá'ís had just completed their Six Year Plan. Shoghi Effendi had praised their achievement, especially the number of Bahá'ís who had arisen to take part, a record in participation for the Formative Age. At Riḍván 1950, with his praise still ringing in their ears, they heard his new summons: a Two Year Plan (1951-53) to plant the banner of the Faith amidst the tribes of central and western Africa. The northern and southern fringes of this vast continent had been illuminated in the course of the Ministries of Bahá'u'lláh and 'Abdu'l-Bahá. The new campaign was designed to eventually carry the light of the Faith to all regions. America was asked especially to send its "dearly beloved members belonging to the Negro race" to pioneer.[27] Britain, Egypt, and Persia sent pioneers. India's part was to consolidate Zanzibar and Madagascar. Five countries thus worked together to take the Faith of Bahá'u'lláh to the tribes of Africa in the first truly international teaching plan.

One of the first pioneers to arise from Persia was Músá Banání, later named a Hand of the Cause of God and the "spiritual conqueror" of Africa.[28] An Assembly was formed in Kampala, Uganda, in 1952. West Africa was opened. Shoghi Effendi increased the goals to twenty-five states and dependencies. By the next year all goals were exceeded. Native African believers arose to teach their people, to pioneer, to go outside their own territories—among them a future Hand of the Cause, Enoch Olinga. Shoghi Effendi later bestowed upon him the honorific "Abu'l-Fútḥ" (the Father of Victories).

DEVELOPMENTS AT THE WORLD CENTER

As the plans progressed, dramatic changes took place in the Holy Land. The State of Israel was formed in May 1948, under a plan adopted by the General Assembly of the United Nations. Almost immediately a short but intense war broke out. During this time Shoghi Effendi, with his small staff of helpers, steadfastly remained in Haifa, conducting the affairs of the Bahá'í world community.

Through Shoghi Effendi's strenuous efforts over a period of

years, the physical properties and endowments in the Holy Land had greatly increased. The Shrine of the Báb would soon lift its golden dome in the heart of Carmel. New terraces and gardens now adorned the slopes of the Holy Mountain, adjoining the serene memorial gardens that shelter the remains of the Holy Family. Protective gardens had been added to the Shrine of Bahá'u'lláh. Bahjí, Bahá'u'lláh's last residence, had been beautifully restored by Shoghi Effendi after he had been able, in 1932, to remove Muḥammad 'Alí and his family from this sacred house they had so pitifully neglected. Mazra'ih, outside 'Akká, where the Manifestation of God had dwelt for a time, was leased in 1950. Now in Bahá'í custody, it was furnished simply and restored in anticipation of future Bahá'í pilgrimage.

All this and much more was achieved by the beloved Guardian alone, over a period of years, in the face of constant opposition and harassment by both old and new Covenant-breakers. They attempted to thwart him in every way they could, slandered his station, wrongly portrayed him to the authorities, and brought legal actions against him. Often his "heavy ladened heart" would turn to the believers for consolation, and they responded with an abundant love and loyalty.[29] In the 1950s, as though God had totally wearied of their presence in the precincts of His Holy Mountain, forces arose to demolish one by one the schemes of the Covenant-breakers. Within a few years, after a "steady decline" in their fortunes, these thorns were finally removed.[30] Houses where they had dwelt near the holy sites were quickly replaced with stately gardens designed by Shoghi Effendi.

APPOINTMENT OF THE INTERNATIONAL BAHÁ'Í COUNCIL. On January 9, 1951, Shoghi Effendi made the historic announcement that he had appointed the International Bahá'í Council, "the first embryonic International Institution," of the Bahá'í world.[31] Including later appointments, its members were: Amatu'l-Bahá Rúḥíyyih Khánum (liaison between the Guardian and the Council), Mason Remey (president), Amelia Collins (vice-president), Leroy Ioas (secretary-general), Jessie Revell (treasurer), Ugo Giachery (member-at-large), Ethel Revell and Luṭfu'lláh Ḥakím (Western and Eastern secretaries), and Sylvia Ioas (appointed in 1955). In the future this Council would become an elected body,

The Second Epoch of the Formative Age   41

Shoghi Effendi stated, and its destiny was to evolve into The Universal House of Justice.

The Council assisted the Guardian in building the Shrine of the Báb, extending the property near the Holy Places, securing the site of the future House of Worship on Mount Carmel, and in cementing relationships with the Israeli Government. The State of Israel, which was itself taking shape during these years, came to recognize the Bahá'í Faith as an independent world religion with both its spiritual and administrative centers in the Holy Land. A special department for Bahá'í affairs was opened in the Ministry for Religious Affairs.

APPOINTMENT OF THE HANDS OF THE CAUSE OF GOD. A cable from the Guardian on December 24, 1951, announced the appointment of the first contingent of Hands of the Cause of God. Both Bahá'u'lláh and 'Abdu'l-Bahá had named certain believers Hands of the Cause. In His Will and Testament the Master had explained that their duties were *"to diffuse the Divine Fragrances, to edify the souls of men, to promote learning, to improve the character of all men"* and to be *"ever watchful"* in protecting the Faith from evil-wishers.[32] Although Shoghi Effendi had given this high rank to certain believers after they had passed on, no appointments had been previously announced.* The Hands of the Cause were to function on all the continents and from the Holy Land. To further their work continental funds were later established, to which Assemblies and individuals were invited to contribute.

Nineteen Hands of the Cause—some already members of the Bahá'í Council—were appointed in two groups over a two-month period. They were William Sutherland Maxwell, Mason Remey, Amelia Collins (in the Holy Land); Valíyu'lláh Varqá, Ṭarázu'lláh Samandarí, 'Alí-Akbar Furútan, Shu'á'u'lláh 'Alá'í, and Dhikru'lláh Khádem (in Persia); George Townshend, Hermann Grossmann, Ugo Giachery, and Adelbert Mühlschlegel (in

---

*See Beatrice Ashton, "Amelia Collins: 1873-1962," in *The Bahá'í World: An International Record, Volume XIII, 1954-1963*, comp. The Universal House of Justice (Haifa: The Universal House of Justice, 1970), pp. 838-39, for details on Shoghi Effendi's unannounced appointment of Amelia Collins as a Hand of the Cause of God in January 1947.

Europe); Horace Holley, Dorothy Baker, Leroy Ioas, Fred Schopflocher, Corinne True (in America); Músá Banání (in Africa); and Clara Dunn (in Australia).

A NEW PLAN FORESHADOWED

As the Holy Year drew near, the teaching plans of the National Assemblies were nearing completion. Shoghi Effendi announced that four Hands of the Cause would represent him at the Intercontinental Conferences to be held in 1953: Leroy Ioas (at the conference in Africa, in February); Rúḥíyyih Khánum, who had been appointed a Hand of the Cause after the passing of her father William Sutherland Maxwell in 1952, accompanied by Amelia Collins (at the conference in America, at Riḍván); Ugo Giachery (at the conference in Europe, in July) and Mason Remey (at the conference in Asia, in October). All were members of the Bahá'í Council.

For some years the Guardian's letters had revealed exciting glimpses of a new teaching plan that would encircle the globe. Pilgrims returned home aglow with what they heard at the Guardian's table. Like a drumbeat drawing nearer, news of this plan began to stir the hearts of the believers, who were still engaged in winning the current goals. It was envisaged as a third Seven Year Plan to begin in 1956. In the spring of 1952 the National Spiritual Assembly of the United States cabled the Guardian expressing a desire not to make use of the promised three-year respite originally mentioned by him, and Shoghi Effendi cabled back his appreciation of this "noble determination."[33]

In spite of forewarning no message from Shoghi Effendi so electrified the Bahá'í world as the one published as *Launching the World-Embracing Spiritual Crusade*.[34] With it he opened the Holy Year in October 1952, announcing the Crusade that would reach throughout the planet and harness the forces of the entire Bahá'í world. Through the years Shoghi Effendi had prepared Bahá'u'lláh's "army of light" for this spiritual conquest of the world.[35] The Hands of the Cause would be the "standard-bearers" of this mighty campaign.[36] To assist them in their work the Hands would appoint during Riḍván 1954 five Auxiliary Boards, one for each continent. The "generals" would be the twelve existing National Assemblies: the British Isles; the United States; Germany and Austria; Egypt and Sudan; 'Iráq; India, Pakistan, and Burma; Persia; Australia and New Zealand; Canada; Central America; South America; Italy and Switzerland.[37] Like a brilliant commander, Shoghi Effendi marshaled the forces of the entire Bahá'í world and launched them on this "soul-stirring, . . . world-embracing Spiritual Crusade."[38]

The fourfold purpose of the plan was (1) development of the World Center, (2) strengthening the national bases from which the twelve plans—one for each National Assembly—would proceed, (3) consolidation of all new territories, and (4) opening the remaining virgin territories. With its details spread out, the scope of this new plan was breathtaking. It included the formation of forty-eight new National Spiritual Assemblies, each to have its own headquarters, constitution, endowment, and legal incorporation; the erection of two new Temples, one in Asia (Persia) and one in Europe (Germany); the purchase of eleven Temple sites and the opening of new countries and territories. Ties with the United Nations were to be strengthened. A beautiful new International Archives building would be built on Mount Carmel, on the "arc" laid out by the Guardian as the site of future edifices for institutions of the World Order of Bahá'u'lláh.[39] Six publishing trusts would be formed and literature published in ninety-one new languages. Precious historic sites in Persia would be secured. And, God willing, the Most Great Jubilee would be celebrated in the vicinity of Baghdád itself.

THE HOLY YEAR AND THE GREAT JUBILEE

African Bahá'ís from thirty tribes, with Orientals and Occidentals from all continents, gathered together literally within a tent of oneness in Kampala. The Hand of the Cause of God Leroy Ioas welcomed them in the Guardian's name, read his message of praise and gratitude for past victories, and outlined the plan for opening the continent of Africa and its islands. Nine other Hands of the Cause were there, touching the hearts of the Africans with stories from the Heroic Age of the Faith and encouraging them to teach and to embrace the administration of their new Faith. The great victory in Africa was winning the hearts of the Africans. Centuries of fear and mistrust were wiped away with tears of joy and love: everyone there knew he was a child of God and an heir of the Kingdom of Bahá'u'lláh. The All-America Conference in Wilmette at Riḍván 1953 was a "triple celebration—the dedication of the Mother Temple of the West, the launching of a World Spiritual Crusade and the commemoration of the Birth of Bahá'u'lláh's Mission."[40] Some twenty-three hundred Bahá'ís heard Rúḥíyyih Khánum read the Guardian's messages and witnessed the dedication of the Temple whose site the Master had blessed forty-one years before. Some were present who had been with the Master that day: one of them was Hand of the Cause of God Valíyu'lláh Varqá, whose father and brother had been martyred in Persia. Bahá'u'lláh's portrait was formally shown for the first time outside the Holy Land. The model of the Temple to adorn Mount Carmel was displayed. The vast goals for America, extending throughout all continents and islands, were disclosed. Pioneers arose by the score. A few weeks after this conference the Guardian announced a Roll of Honor for the "Knights of Bahá'u'lláh," those pioneers who would open the virgin territories.[41] It was later to be placed, he said, beneath the entrance of the Tomb of Bahá'u'lláh.

Fourteen Hands of the Cause, the largest number at any of the conferences, were present at the Stockholm conference convened by the European Teaching Committee of America. The Hand of the Cause of God Ugo Giachery pinpointed the most immediate goals on which to begin work: building the Temple in Frankfurt, opening the virgin territories, acquiring the Temple sites in Rome and Stockholm, and translating urgently needed literature. Before the conference closed, pioneers had volunteered for all the European territories.

The New Delhi conference held in October closed the Holy Year. Here the Faith achieved a new prestige as the president of the Indian Republic, His Excellency Dr. Rajendra Prasad, opened the conference and declared it a unique event for the Orient, with its wide display of racial and cultural backgrounds. Special Bahá'í delegations called upon the president and vice-president of India, as well as Prime Minister Nehru. The Hand of the Cause Clara

Dunn encouraged the seventy-four pioneers who arose with these words: " 'If we have faith we can conquer the whole world.' "⁴² Following the conference the Hands of the Cause who had been present carried out, at Shoghi Effendi's request, teaching journeys throughout Asia, Africa, and Australasia.

A highlight of all the conferences was the Guardian's comprehensive world survey of the Faith from 1844 to 1952 and detailed charting of the new plan. His colorful map depicted the goals of the twelve National Spiritual Assemblies and helped Bahá'ís to grasp this awe-inspiring, world-embracing plan.⁴³

THE TEN YEAR WORLD CRUSADE (1953-1963)

"When we look back a hundred years ago," said the Hand of the Cause of God Dhikru'lláh Khádem at the Stockholm conference, "Bahá'u'lláh was alone [in the Síyáh-Chál], but now His lovers all around the world, in twenty-five hundred localities in one hundred twenty-nine countries speak of Him in ninety different languages!"⁴⁴ Looking ahead ten years, the lovers of Bahá'u'lláh would be calling His name in over eleven thousand localities and in more than three hundred languages!

The Ten Year Crusade is a story filled with heroism, love, and sacrifice—and with deep sorrow. Above all, it is the story of a great victory won by the Bahá'ís through steadfast faith in Bahá'u'lláh and in the guidance of Shoghi Effendi. The first phase of the plan, covering a year, saw the opening of a hundred countries and territories from the Arctic Circle to the Indian Ocean. Only eight virgin goals remained to be opened, apart from those places where political conditions prevented the entry of pioneers.

At this time the Bahá'ís in the cradle of the Faith were steadily building up their Temple Fund and acquiring the sites of historic significance to the Faith. The Síyáh-Chál, loathsome dungeon where once the Manifestation of God had been held in chains, was acquired in 1954. Then, in 1955, without warning, a shattering blow was struck against the Persian believers. Bahá'ís were killed, their property seized, crops destroyed, the teachings distorted in the press, and the dome of the beautiful national Ḥaẓíratu'l-Quds in Ṭihrán demolished. This vicious attack, spurred on by fanatical religous leaders, came as a shock to many people in the world, as well as to the Bahá'ís. Under the Guardian's direction the Bahá'í world rallied immediately to the support of their assailed brothers and sisters. Appeals were directed to the sháh and to the Iranian Parliament and registered with the United Nations. World leaders raised their voices in protest—Eleanor Roosevelt, Pandit Nehru, and Professor Arnold Toynbee, to name a few. The secretary-general of the United Nations sent a representative to the Iranian delegate to confer on the matter and seek redress. The persecution began to diminish, although it would take two years and another appeal to the United Nations to bring it to a halt. For the first time an attack upon the Bahá'ís in Persia had come to the attention of the whole world, including its highest seat of justice. It was, in effect, a wide proclamation of the Faith of Bahá'u'lláh. The building of the Temple in Persia, however, had to be postponed. Shortly thereafter Shoghi Effendi announced that, instead, two Temples would rise, one in the heart of Africa, in Kampala, and one in Australasia, in Sydney.

By Riḍván 1956 the Faith had reached 247 countries and major territories. The Guardian considered it a "major turning point" in the Crusade. He discerned signs "in far-off regions heralding the approach of the day when troops will flock" to the standard of the Faith.[45] He encouraged "the warriors enlisting under its banner" in these words: "Putting on the armor of His love, firmly buckling on the shield of His mighty Covenant, mounted on the steed of steadfastness, holding aloft the lance of the Word of the Lord of Hosts, and with unquestioning reliance on His promises as the best provision for their journey, let them set their faces towards the fields that still remain unexplored and direct their steps to those goals that are as yet unattained, assured that He Who has led them to achieve such triumphs, and to store up such prizes in His Kingdom, will continue to assist them in enriching their spiritual birthright to a degree that no finite mind can imagine or human heart perceive."[46]

The increase in the number of National and Regional Assemblies began at Riḍván 1956 with three additional ones in Africa, making four in all. Latin America expanded from two to four Assemblies in 1957. New National Assemblies were formed in

South East Asia, North East Asia, the Arabian Peninsula, Alaska, New Zealand, and Pakistan, as well as three in Western Europe. Fourteen new pillars of the future Universal House of Justice had been raised. The Guardian's 1952 Riḍván message, listing many victories, was filled with joy. He was moved to prepare a new map detailing the achievements, many far beyond the original scope of the Plan.[47]

His message of June 4, 1957, asked the Hands of the Cause to assume their "primary obligation to watch over" and protect the Bahá'í community, as well as to prosecute the World Crusade, in close collaboration with the National Assemblies.[48] In October he appointed eight more Hands of the Cause, making a total of twenty-seven: Enoch Olinga, William Sears, and John Robarts (in Africa); Ḥasan Balyuzi and John Ferraby (in the British Isles); Collis Featherstone and Raḥmatu'lláh Muhájir (in the Pacific), and Abu'l-Qásim Faizí (in the Arabian Peninsula).

Since earlier appointees William Sutherland Maxwell, Siegfried Schopflocher, Dorothy Baker, Valíyu'lláh Varqá, and George Townshend had passed away, they were replaced by Rúḥíyyih Khánum, 1952; Jalál Kházeh, 1953; Paul Haney, 1954; 'Alí-Muḥammad Varqá, 1955; and Agnes Alexander, 1957.

October 1957 brought the good news from the Guardian that five Intercontinental Conferences would be held in 1958, the midpoint of the Crusade, to give thanks to Bahá'u'lláh and to consult on remaining goals. In this, his last letter to the Bahá'ís of the world, Shoghi Effendi designated the Hands of the Cause as the "Chief Stewards of Bahá'u'lláh's embryonic World Commonwealth," a mandate whose incalculable blessings were so shortly and so tragically to appear.[49] The last half of this plan, he stated, must be marked by the entry of large numbers of believers into the Cause. He concluded the letter with a plea for all Bahá'ís to "bestir themselves [toward] . . . hastening the establishment of His Kingdom in the hearts of men."[50]

THE PASSING OF SHOGHI EFFENDI

These were Shoghi Effendi's last words to his followers around the globe. On November 4 came a heartbreaking cable from

Rúḥíyyih Khánum: the Guardian had passed away suddenly in London. The beloved commander of Bahá'u'lláh's "Army of Light" had fallen. Stunned, grief stricken, the Bahá'ís who had followed him trustingly into every unknown field gathered in London as this *"priceless pearl"* given to them by the Master was laid to rest.[51] Only those who remembered the Master's passing thirty-six years earlier could compare the sorrow. Yet, after the first shock and grief had subsided, the Bahá'ís returned to their tasks, assured by those Chief Stewards, the Hands of the Cause, and moved by the courageous example of Rúḥíyyih Khánum.

The first of the five conferences opened two months later in Kampala with Rúḥíyyih Khánum as the Guardian's chosen representative. Conferences followed in Sydney, in March, with Mason Remey; in Chicago, in May, with Ugo Giachery; in Frankfurt, in July, with Amelia Collins; and in Singapore (where it had to be moved from Djakarta at the last moment), in September, with Leroy Ioas. Each conference received precious gifts that Shoghi Effendi himself previously arranged—the blessed portraits to view, earth from the Shrine of Bahá'u'lláh for Temple foundation ceremonies in Kampala and Sydney, and the Guardian's mid-Crusade map, so recently come from his hands. The Bahá'ís vowed to bring complete victory in the name of the Guardian by April 1963.

THE HANDS OF THE CAUSE OF GOD AS CHIEF STEWARDS

The Hands of the Cause of God gathered in the Holy Land immediately following the passing of Shoghi Effendi and issued a proclamation on November 25 informing the Bahá'í world that Shoghi Effendi had left no heir and had appointed no Guardian to succeed him. Nine Hands were chosen to remain at the World Center. The proclamation was signed by twenty-six Hands of the Cause, Mrs. Corinne True, ninety-six years old, not being present. The major task for Bahá'ís now was to complete the goals of the Crusade. The Hands of the Cause held a conclave in the Holy Land each autumn, from 1958 through 1962, and in the spring of 1963, and informed the Bahá'ís of developments throughout each year. Most of the Hands traveled ceaselessly now, encouraging the

The Second Epoch of the Formative Age 49

believers in their work, and giving of themselves in full measure. The blessing Bahá'u'lláh had conferred upon the Hands of the Cause in the Tablet to the World—those *"through whom the light of fortitude hath shone forth and the truth hath been established that the authority to choose rests with God"*—took on deeper meaning.[52] The defection of Mason Remey in April 1960, through his claim to be the "hereditary Guardian," failed to create division in the Faith. He was expelled from the ranks of the faithful, along with his few, misguided followers. He spent his last days in obscurity, unrepentant and abandoned by nearly all his erstwhile followers. Before the completion of the World Crusade four Hands of the Cause passed away: Horace Holley (1960) and Amelia Collins (1962) in the Holy Land, Clara Dunn (1960) in Australia, and Corinne True (1961) in the United States.

THE ELECTION OF THE INTERNATIONAL BAHÁ'Í COUNCIL

The Hands of the Cause called for the election of the International Bahá'í Council at Riḍván 1961, in accordance with the instructions of Shoghi Effendi concerning this stage of the Council's development.[53] In this first Bahá'í election on a world scale, the National Spiritual Assemblies of the world cast their ballots by mail and elected the following members: Jessie Revell, 'Alí Nakhjavání, Luṭfu'lláh Ḥakím, Ethel Revell, Charles Wolcott, Sylvia Ioas, Mildred Mottahedeh, Ian Semple, and H. Borrah Kavelin. The newly elected Council continued the work of the former Council, with various added duties. It assisted Amatu'l-Bahá Rúḥíyyih Khánum to complete the furnishing and arrangement of the International Archives building in 1961 so that it could be opened for pilgrims. When the Hands of the Cause determined that the Bahá'í World Congress could not be held in Baghdád and announced that the site of this great gathering of Bahá'ís would be London, the Council, assisted by a committee in England, assumed the work of preparing for this Most Great Jubilee.

The Crusade forged ahead. Rúḥíyyih Khánum dedicated the Temples in Kampala and Sydney in January and in September

1961.* More National Spiritual Assemblies were formed: France, in 1958; Austria, Burma, Turkey, and the South Pacific Islands, in 1959; and twenty-one Latin American republics and the Antilles, in 1961. Only the eleven Western European Assemblies and Ceylon remained to be elected in 1962.

THE HISTORIC FIRST ELECTION OF THE UNIVERSAL HOUSE OF JUSTICE

From the beginning of his Guardianship Shoghi Effendi pointed the sights of the Bahá'ís toward the future establishment of The Universal House of Justice, which Bahá'u'lláh had ordained in His Most Holy Book, and which 'Abdu'l-Bahá had described in His Will and Testament as the "*source of all good and freed from all error.*"[54] Each new National Spiritual Assembly became one more pillar to "share in sustaining the weight and in broadening the foundation of the Universal House of Justice," which, along with its "manifold auxiliary institutions" was "destined to arise and function and remain permanently established in [the] close neighborhood of [the] Twin Holy Shrines."[55]

As Riḍván 1963 approached, the International Bahá'í Council, first appointed by the Guardian, then elected by the National Spiritual Assemblies in 1961, was about to effloresce into The Universal House of Justice.[56] Five hundred four delegates from fifty-six National and Regional Spiritual Assemblies participated in the election, of whom 288 delegates from fifty-one National Assemblies assembled in the Holy Land in April when the election of this supreme administrative institution of the Bahá'í world took place.

The members elected to this first Universal House of Justice were: Charles Wolcott, 'Alí Nakhjavání, H. Borrah Kavelin, Ian Semple, Luṭfu'lláh Ḥakím, David Hofman, Hugh Chance, Amoz Gibson, and Hushmand Fatheazam. The Hands of the Cause joyously cabled the news to all National Assemblies. It was the

---

*The Mother Temple of Europe in Frankfurt-am-Main, Germany, almost completed by the end of the World Crusade, was dedicated by Rúḥíyyih Khánum in July 1964.

The Second Epoch of the Formative Age 51

crowning achievement of a magnificent epoch—the first epoch of the Divine Plan, and the second of the Formative Age.[57]

THE BAHÁ'Í WORLD CONGRESS
(APRIL 28-MAY 2, 1963)

Nearly seven thousand jubilant Bahá'ís gathered in London to observe the centenary of Bahá'u'lláh's Declaration in the Garden of Riḍván, near Baghdád, and to pay homage to their beloved Guardian at his resting place. The newly elected Universal House of Justice greeted the believers who had laid "this glorious harvest of victory" in the World Crusade, in the name of the Guardian, "at the feet of the Blessed Beauty." They expressed "profound admiration for the heroic work" of the Hands of the Cause, acknowledging "the reality of the sacrifice, the labor, the self-discipline, the superb stewardship" of these chief stewards of the Faith who had "kept the ship on its course and brought it safe to port."[58]

It seemed as if the whole human race, like a flower garden of humanity, were represented at the London Congress. The London press bore witness to the blend of races, nationalities, and costumes and to the warm fellowship that so colorfully marked this Most Great Jubilee. Bahá'ís listened to remembrances of Shoghi Effendi tenderly shared by Rúḥíyyih Khánum and by the other Hands of the Cause who were present. Victories were recounted, the Riḍván Feast was celebrated, and songs were sung by the African friends—all to become memories forever engraved upon the hearts. The most sacred moment for each believer was a visit to the beloved Guardian's grave, now adorned with its marble column, globe, and golden eagle. Only the knowledge that several fellow Bahá'ís were held in a Moroccan prison, some condemned to death for their belief in Bahá'u'lláh, marred the joy of the believers. It would be eight more months before the good news of their release would come.

Now all three of the Divine Charters were in effect.* The supreme administrative body, The Universal House of Justice,

---
*See "Three Divine Charters," pp. 2-3.

was seated in the Holy Land. The Divine Plan had been carried forward to the continents and islands, and a strong administrative foundation had been laid on the base of fifty-six National Spiritual Assemblies, an increase of forty-four in ten years.[59] Deep assurance filled the hearts of the believers as they left this Congress under the protective wings of their Universal House of Justice, ready to follow its lead for the "onward march of the Cause."[60]

The Third Epoch of the Formative Age

A NEW, NINE YEAR PLAN

When the Ten Year Crusade had opened, Shoghi Effendi described ten separate stages of the vast "majestic process" for the salvation of mankind "set in motion at the dawn of the Adamic cycle." The first part was the six thousand year Prophetic Cycle from Adam to the Báb. This was a preparatory stage, "the slow and steady growth of this tree of divine revelation," given to mankind through a "series of progressive dispensations, associated with Moses, Zoroaster, Buddha, Jesus, Muḥammad and other Prophets." The next six stages covered the Heroic Age of the Bahá'í Faith. Two of these stages were the mission and martyrdom of the Báb, and Bahá'u'lláh's mission in Ṭihrán, Baghdád, Adrianople, and 'Akká, which brought the Faith to 13 countries in the Asiatic and African continents. The Ministry of 'Abdu'l-Bahá was the seventh stage, at which time the light of the Faith reached Europe and the Americas and included more than 30 countries. The eighth stage covering the first thirty-two years of the Formative Age to 1953, brought the Faith to 128 countries and marked the beginning, in 1937, of the systematic prosecution of the Divine Plan. The Ten Year Crusade alone, during which time the number of countries and major territories opened to the Faith doubled, was the ninth stage in this drama of salvation. The tenth stage, Shoghi Effendi stated, would extend far into the future and would include many worldwide plans. It would lead to the Golden Age and to that "long-awaited advent of the Christ-promised Kingdom of God on earth," and to a "world civilization, incomparable in its range, its character and potency, in the history of mankind."[1]

The tenth part of this vast "majestic process" began when The Universal House of Justice announced a new Nine Year Plan to begin at Riḍván 1964 and to end with the hundredth anniversary of the revelation of the Kitáb-i-Aqdas in 1973. It twin objectives were widespread expansion of the Cause and universal participation. The goals included opening seventy virgin territories, raising the number of National Assemblies to 108 (later increased to 113), and the number of Local Assemblies to fourteen thousand, building two Temples (Panama and Ṭihrán), acquiring sixty-two Temple sites and fifty-two national Ḥaẓíratu'l-Quds. The number of schools, publishing trusts, and translations would all be greatly augmented. World Center goals involved further strengthening of the relationship with the United Nations, the development of the institution of the Hands of the Cause with a view to the extension into the future of their appointed functions of protection and propagation, and the development of the physical properties at the World Center.[2]

Universal participation could be achieved and bring "a source of power and vitality as yet unknown to us," the Supreme Body advised, if every Bahá'í would teach the Cause, try to live up to its laws and standards, contribute to the Fund, and strive to deepen his understanding of Bahá'u'lláh's Revelation. "All can pray, fight their own spiritual battles, and contribute to the Fund."[3]

The hundredth year of Bahá'u'lláh's Proclamation from Adrianople to the kings and rulers of the world would be observed through a number of intercontinental and oceanic conferences, The Universal House of Justice announced.

WORLDWIDE PROCLAMATION

A vital part of this new plan quickly became evident: teaching among the masses of humanity, the unsophisticated and unlettered souls who make up the majority of the world's peoples. The entry of "troops" promised by the Master had begun in East Africa even before the Ten Year Plan.[4] It spread in the 1960s to the Congo, to Southeast Asia, to a number of Pacific Island groups and to Bolivia. India enrolled over thirty thousand believers between Riḍván and November 1962. By the start of the Nine Year Plan the flame was spreading to many lands. The Guajiros of Colombia and Venezuela, the Mayans of Yucatan (Mexico), tribes in the jungles

The Third Epoch of the Formative Age   55

of Brazil and elsewhere in Latin America, as well as the *campesinos* (country people), in large numbers showed an eagerness to embrace the Cause. West Africa awakened, numbers of Bahá'ís enrolling first in the Cameroons and Nigeria. In all these areas the believers were greatly inspired by visits of the Hands of the Cause and their Auxiliary Board members who encouraged the Bahá'ís to reach the villages and people removed from large centers of civilization.

The Universal House of Justice called upon Bahá'í youth throughout the world to plan their education and their lives toward service to the Faith, to participate fully in community life, and especially to learn the "wonderful skill of Bahá'í consultation." ". . . the achievements of Bahá'í youth," wrote the House of Justice in 1966, "are increasingly advancing the work of the Nine Year Plan."[5]

A new dimension for spreading the Faith was opened by the Supreme Body—worldwide proclamation. As an exile in Turkey Bahá'u'lláh had fearlessly proclaimed His Faith to the powerful rulers of His day. Now the time had come to proclaim it to "every stratum of human society."[6] The six Intercontinental Conferences held in October 1967 put this heightened dimension into motion. *The Proclamation of Bahá'u'lláh*, compiled and published by The Universal House of Justice, was presented on its behalf to heads of state around the world.[7] National and Local Assemblies continued the process on other levels.

The observance of the hundredth anniversary of the revelation of Bahá'u'lláh's Tablets to the Kings began in Adrianople at the site of His House where the "most momentous Tablet" had been revealed.[8] Six Hands of the Cause met there on behalf of The Universal House of Justice and then dispersed to the six conferences. To each conference they carried a special message from the Supreme Body for the assembled believers. The Hand of the Cause Amatu'l-Bahá Rúḥíyyih Khánum laid the foundation stone of the Temple in Panama, with over two hundred Indian Bahá'ís from many tribes lending a special grace and color to the event. Native music with the heartbeat of Africa welcomed the Hand of the Cause 'Alí-Akbar Furútan and other Bahá'ís to Kampala. India did its usual masterful job of contacting national leaders, aided by the

Hand of the Cause of God Abu'l-Qásim Faizí. The lord mayor of Sydney opened the Australian conference with a reception honoring the Hand of the Cause Ugo Giachery and other Bahá'ís. African, Middle and Far Eastern, North and South American faces all blended with their European brothers and sisters at the Frankfurt conference to greet the Hand of the Cause of God Paul Haney. "The time is ripe," The Universal House of Justice declared. "We are not alone nor helpless. . . . the 'army of Light' can achieve such victories as will astonish posterity."[9]

The Hand of the Cause of God Ṭarázu'lláh Samandarí, ninety-two years of age, shared his memories of Bahá'u'lláh at the Chicago conference and with amazing power poured forth loving exhortation to the believers. He followed this with a journey throughout North America through many harsh and changing climates. Leading religious journalists across the land were drawn to him, and remarkable publicity resulted. It seemed a special gift of Providence to this heroic standard-bearer of the Cause that he was able to lay down his banner for all time in the Holy Land while Bahá'ís from all over the world assembled, in August 1968, to observe the centenary of Bahá'u'lláh's journey to 'Akká.

This Holy Land observance was held immediately following the first Oceanic Conference, in Palermo, Sicily, which commemorated Bahá'u'lláh's voyage across the Mediterranean Sea to the Most Great Prison.

The second International Bahá'í Convention elected Dr. David Ruhe to The Universal House of Justice. Luṭfu'lláh Ḥakím had resigned his membership before the election due to reasons of health. Dr. Ḥakím, who had served both the Master and the Guardian for many years in the Holy Land, passed away in August a few weeks prior to the centenary event there.

APPOINTMENT OF THE
CONTINENTAL BOARDS OF COUNSELORS

The Universal House of Justice appointed eleven Continental Boards of Counselors in June 1968: three each in Africa and Asia; one each in North America, Central America, South America,

The Third Epoch of the Formative Age 57

Australasia, and Europe. This historic step was taken to extend into the future the functions of protection and propagation which had been conferred upon the Hands of the Cause, and which would now also be exercised by the Boards of Counselors. The Hands of the Cause in the Holy Land were named as the liaison between the Boards and the House of Justice. Auxiliary Board members were to serve the Counselors, who would appoint them in the future.* The Hands of the Cause were now released from the administrative duties of their institution to carry out special missions for the World Center and to teach throughout all parts of the world. Their continued responsibility to consult with the National Assemblies, as well as with the Counselors, was stressed.

MIDPOINT OF THE PLAN

As the Nine Year Plan reached its midpoint in 1968, The Universal House of Justice published a progress report.[10] Eighty-one of the 113 National Assemblies had been formed. The Faith had reached 314 countries, 135 of these being independent nations. Tribes and minority groups in the Faith had more than doubled since 1963. More than half the teaching institutes called for in the plan had been acquired in the mass-teaching areas.

But the teaching field stretched endlessly; an immense harvest lay waiting. April 1969 brought a call for 733 more pioneers. Youth were entering the Cause in larger numbers, especially in America. Rúhíyyih Khánum interrupted her African teaching journey to meet with more than two thousand American youth gathered in the shadow of the Temple in Wilmette in June 1970. The youth were in the process of fulfilling a Five Year Plan given to them at their own request by the National Assembly of the

---

*For elucidation of the collaborative functioning of the Hands of the Cause of God, the Continental Boards of Counselors, and the Auxiliary Board members, with National and Local Spiritual Assemblies see messages from The Universal House of Justice to the Continental Boards of Counselors and National Spiritual Assemblies, dated October 1, 1969, and April 24, 1972, published in *Messages from The Universal House of Justice: 1968-1973* (Wilmette, Ill.: Bahá'í Publishing Trust, 1976), pp. 29-33, 91-95.

United States. It called for deployment of five hundred from their ranks to fill homefront and foreign goals, doubling the number of Bahá'í college clubs, increasing the number of high school clubs, and engaging in extensive travel-teaching programs. Teaching the masses began to occur in the deep south of the United States and believers enrolled in large numbers.

OCEANIC AND CONTINENTAL CONFERENCES (1970-1971)

Mass teaching was a leading subject at the eight Oceanic and Continental Conferences held in 1970-71. Members of eleven Indian tribes from Surinam to Argentina were among the Bahá'ís who greeted Rúḥíyyih Khánum as representative of The Universal House of Justice at the Bolivian conference in August 1970. The Indian Ocean conference in Mauritius, held at the same time, brought forth, under the inspiration of the Hand of the Cause of God William Sears, a record number of 212 pioneers for Africa. Before their conference in January 1971 Singapore Bahá'ís blanketed their city with half a million pamphlets in three languages and welcomed a first visit from the Hand of the Cause of God Enoch Olinga. Simultaneously, the conference held in Monrovia, Liberia, was highlighted by discussions on mass teaching led by both Rúḥíyyih Khánum and the official representative of the House of Justice, the Hand of the Cause Raḥmatu'lláh Muhájir, each drawing on their wide experience in this field. A cruise ship, which made teaching stops along the way, carried six hundred Bahá'ís from the United States to the Jamaican conference held in May 1971, where the Hand of the Cause Dhikru'lláh Khádem represented The Universal House of Justice. Its counterpart, the Fijian conference, with the Hand of the Cause of God Collis Featherstone as official representative of the House of Justice, was marked by a complete confidence that the Faith would sweep through the farflung scattered islands of the Pacific. The Hand of the Cause of God 'Alí-Akbar Furútan represented The Universal House of Justice at the conference in Sapporo, Japan, in September 1971. A follow-up conference in Korea, with the Hand of the Cause Collis Featherstone present, drew five hundred believers. John Robarts, a

Hand of the Cause of God, read the message from The Universal House of Justice, as its official representative to the Icelandic conference held in Reykjavik, also in September. During the closing days of the Oceanic conferences news came of the passing of the Hand of the Cause Músá Banání, in Africa. Other revered Hands of the Cause who had passed on during the Nine Year Plan were: Leroy Ioas (1965), Ṭarázu'lláh Samandarí (1968), Hermann Grossmann (1968), and Agnes Alexander (1971).

THE TEACHING JOURNEYS OF THE
HAND OF THE CAUSE OF GOD
AMATU'L-BAHÁ RÚḤÍYYIH KHÁNUM

No account of the Nine Year Plan, or indeed of the Formative Age of the Faith, would be complete without a review, however brief, of the epic teaching journeys of the Hand of the Cause Amatu'l-Bahá Rúḥíyyih Khánum. Even prior to the Nine Year Plan, and after the passing of the beloved Guardian, she had made journeys to all continents, inspiring the Bahá'ís; dedicating Temples; meeting presidents, emperors, prime ministers, and other world leaders; and teaching the Cause to people from every walk of life. She taught thousands of unlettered people who were deeply moved by her manner and spirit. Her journey to Asia in 1964 lasted nine months and extended 55,000 miles, by plane, auto, jeep, and boat, and on foot, through India, Ceylon, Nepal, and Sikkim. Hundreds of villages, often difficult to reach, received her visits. Most countries of Latin America and the Caribbean were her hosts during her two conference visits in 1967 and 1970, where again she reached out to the remote areas. On all her journeys she was respectfully received by many outstanding dignitaries and leaders of public opinion and was widely interviewed in the press and on radio and television. Large audiences, often in schools and universities, listened attentively to her addresses on the Faith.

But the crowning glory of her travels was the African Safari, planned during nine years and begun in August 1969. She was accompanied by Violette Nakhjavání, her courageous and devoted companion on many previous journeys. When the tour was completed in January 1973 these intrepid travelers "had driven 36,000 miles by landrover, the majority over expanses which could scarcely qualify for description as roads, flown unnumbered miles by air and voyaged vast distances by watercraft," passing through every conceivable climate and terrain.[11] They had visited more than thirty countries.

In her summary of this great teaching journey Violette Nakhjavání wrote of Rúhíyyih Khánum: "I firmly believe that future generations will study her life, her services and her travels in those lands honoured by her visits, and pattern their conduct on her example, inspired to follow in her footsteps."[12]

Amatu'l-Bahá Rúhíyyih Khánum had taken her leave from the resting place of Shoghi Effendi in London. She returned there at the completion of her African safari to lay her services and her victories at his feet. The Universal House of Justice expressed the grateful appreciation and admiration of the entire Bahá'í world in its cable: "Your travels African continent unique unparalleled in number countries visited heads state interviewed extensive publicity obtained loving encouragement spiritual stimulation imparted standard heroism example selfsacrifice evinced over such long period under such arduous conditions."[13] She returned to the Holy Land in time to open the third International Bahá'í Convention held at Riḍván 1973, which also marked the triumphant conclusion of the Nine Year Plan.

THE CONCLUSION OF THE NINE YEAR PLAN

"A new horizon, bright with intimations of thrilling developments in the unfolding life of the Cause of God, is now discernible," wrote The Universal House of Justice at Riḍván 1971. "We are confident that the Army of Light, growing in strength and unity will, by 1973, . . . have scaled the heights of yet another peak in the path leading ultimately to the broad uplands of the Most Great Peace."[14]

A review of the first half century of the Formative Age would fall short of its purpose if it failed to record the significant accom-

The Third Epoch of the Formative Age 61

plishments of the Bahá'í Faith in the last years of the Nine Year Plan. The concluding years of this second global campaign, the first inaugurated by The Universal House of Justice, were filled with momentous events that exhilarated the hearts of believers throughout the world. It had surpassed its goals for expansion and "achieved a truly impressive degree of universal participation."[15] The systematic formation of National Spiritual Assemblies culminated in a final 113, exceeding the goal of 108. Ninety of these achieved incorporation, and 112 acquired their national headquarters. Bahá'ís were now spread throughout almost seventy thousand localities of the world. They had established over seventeen thousand Local Spiritual Assemblies. The Faith had penetrated 335 countries, significant territories, and islands—a gain of 95 in nine years. The number of publishing trusts, national endowments, Temple sites, and translations had approximately doubled.

The spirit animating the Bahá'í community was most vividly demonstrated in the response made to the call for pioneers: a total of 1,344 had been called for—3,553 responded; 2,265 were still at their posts as the plan concluded.

The Universal House of Justice named three "highly portentous developments" resulting from the nine year campaign: the large number of inter-National Assembly assistance projects carried out which had served "to strengthen the bonds of unity between distant parts of the Bahá'í world with different social, cultural and historical backgrounds"; the "vast increase in the financial resources of the Faith"; and the advance of youth to the forefront of the teaching work.[16] This spiritual vitality of the youth was abundantly evident at a conference in Fiesch, Switzerland, in the summer of 1971. It drew twelve hundred youth from five continents who were not only inspired by the Hands of the Cause Amatu'l-Bahá Rúḥíyyih Khánum and Dr. Adelbert Mühlschlegel but succeeded in making a far-reaching proclamation of the Faith.

The fiftieth anniversary of the passing of 'Abdu'l-Bahá was observed throughout the Bahá'í world in November 1971, poignancy being lent by the presence of believers who had met the Master. A few weeks later, on December 19, The Universal House of Justice shared news of the erection of an obelisk on Mount

Carmel to mark the site of the future Mashriqu'l-Adhkár, a project initiated by Shoghi Effendi.

In April 1972 Rúḥíyyih Khánum again interrupted her African journey to officiate at the dedication of the first House of Worship in Latin America in Panama. The Hand of the Cause Dhikru'lláh Khádem and four thousand other Bahá'ís participated in the dedication ceremonies, public meetings, banquets, and a two-day teaching conference. One month later Bahá'ís were apprised of plans for the construction of a majestic edifice on Mount Carmel—a building to serve as the permanent seat of The Universal House of Justice. A special fund was established for the participation of all believers.

November 26, 1972, brought news of great, historic import to the world community of Bahá'ís: the formulation of the Constitution of The Universal House of Justice, hailed, in anticipation, by Shoghi Effendi as the Most Great Law of the Faith of Bahá'u'lláh. The publication of *A Synopsis and Codification of the Laws and Ordinances of the Kitáb-i-Aqdas* coincided with the centenary of the revelation of this Most Holy Book of Bahá'u'lláh and was described by the Supreme Body as ''another significant step path leading Bahá'í community full maturity establishment World Order Bahá'u'lláh.''[17]

The Bahá'ís experienced special joy in learning that the Mansion of Mazra'ih, cherished home of Bahá'u'lláh for two years after leaving the prison city of 'Akká, had been purchased. This Mansion, one of twin historic Houses inhabited by Bahá'u'lláh, had been leased by Shoghi Effendi in 1950 and made a place of pilgrimage. Additional land was now acquired, and plans were made to beautify the surrounding area.

A few days following the third International Convention, which resulted in the reelection of the nine members of The Universal House of Justice, this body released the news of an event that crowned all the victories of the Nine Year Plan. A reigning monarch, His Highness Malietoa Tanumafili II, the head of state of the independent nation of Western Samoa, had accepted the Faith of Bahá'u'lláh. His letter addressed to those assembled at the convention in the Holy Land expressed his cherished hope ''for the rapid establishment of the Kingdom of God on earth and the unity of all the peoples of the world."[18]

THE ESTABLISHMENT OF THE INTERNATIONAL TEACHING CENTER IN THE HOLY LAND

A cable of June 5, 1973, from The Universal House of Justice announced the establishment of the International Teaching Center in the Holy Land, one of the institutions "'ordained by Bahá'u'lláh anticipated by 'Abdu'l-Bahá elucidated by Shoghi Effendi."[19] This act brought to fruition the work of the Hands of the Cause residing in the Holy Land, provided for its extension into the future, linked the institution of the Boards of Counselors more intimately with that of the Hands of the Cause of God, and powerfully reinforced the discharge of the rapidly growing responsibilities of The Universal House of Justice.

Although all the Hands of the Cause of God are included in the membership of the International Teaching Center, most of them are occupied with service in other parts of the globe. It was, therefore, decided that there should be a nucleus in the Holy Land to carry on the vital operations at the World Center. This nucleus is composed of any Hands present in the Holy Land at any time, together with three Counselors appointed to the body—Mr. Hooper Dunbar, Mrs. Florence Mayberry, and Mr. 'Azíz Yazdí. The Hands of the Cause residing in the Holy Land—Rúhíyyih Khánum, 'Alí-Akbar Furútan, Paul Haney, and Abu'l-Qásim Faizí—are the ones most usually serving on the nucleus, but other Hands have contributed valuably to its deliberations from time to time when visiting Haifa. The immediate responsibilities of the International Teaching Center are to direct the work of the Continental Boards and act as liaison with The Universal House of Justice; to be informed of the situation of the Cause throughout the world and make reports and recommendations for action; and to determine needs for literature, pioneers, and traveling teachers and to work out teaching plans with the approval of The Universal House of Justice.

The International Teaching Center, destined to evolve into one of those "world shaking world embracing world directing administrative institutions" was now seated in the Holy Land.[20]

GOD'S HOLY PURPOSE FOR MANKIND

The centennial year of the revelation of the Kitáb-i-Aqdas, which had yielded so many historical advances for the Cause of God, climaxed over a half century of the Formative Age of the Bahá'í Faith—a period fraught with many challenges and crises but laden with ultimate victory.

In the early days of the Formative Age, a youthful Guardian wrote to his "Fellow-laborers in the Divine Vineyard" urging them to pray "that in these days of world-encircling gloom, . . . when the most precious fruits of civilization are undergoing severe and unparalleled tests, we may all realize, . . . that though a mere handful amidst the seething masses of the world, we are in this day the chosen instruments of God's grace, that our mission is most urgent and vital to the fate of humanity, and, fortified by these sentiments, arise to achieve God's holy purpose for mankind."[21]

At Riḍván 1973 The Universal House of Justice wrote: "The progress of the Cause of God gathers increasing momentum and we may with confidence look forward to the day when this Community, in God's good time, shall have traversed the stages predicted for it by its Guardian, and shall have raised on this tormented planet the fair mansions of God's Own Kingdom wherein humanity may find surcease from its self-induced confusion and chaos and ruin, and the hatreds and violence of this time shall be transmuted into an abiding sense of world brotherhood and peace. All this shall be accomplished within the Covenant of the everlasting Father, the Covenant of Bahá'u'lláh."[22]

Notes

THE CLOSE OF THE HEROIC AGE

1. Shoghi Effendi, *God Passes By*, rev. ed. (Wilmette, Ill.: Bahá'í Publishing Trust, 1974), p. 324.
2. Shoghi Effendi, *The World Order of Bahá'u'lláh: Selected Letters*, 2d rev. ed. (Wilmette, Ill.: Bahá'í Publishing Trust, 1974), p. 98.
3. Shoghi Effendi, *God Passes By*, p. 140.
4. *A Synopsis and Codification of The Kitáb-i-Aqdas: The Most Holy Book of Bahá'u'lláh*, [comp. The Universal House of Justice], (Haifa: Bahá'í World Centre, 1973) was published in 1973, fulfilling a goal of the Nine Year Plan.
5. 'Abdu'l-Bahá, quoted in Shoghi Effendi, *God Passes By*, p. 238.
6. Bahá'u'lláh, *Gleanings from the Writings of Bahá'u'lláh*, trans. Shoghi Effendi, 2d rev. ed. (Wilmette, Ill.: Bahá'í Publishing Trust, 1976), pp. 14-17.
7. Shoghi Effendi, *The Advent of Divine Justice*, 3d rev. ed. (Wilmette, Ill.: Bahá'í Publishing Trust, 1969), pp. 3-4.
8. 'Abdu'l-Bahá, *Tablets of the Divine Plan: Revealed by 'Abdu'l-Bahá to the North American Bahá'ís*, rev. ed. (Wilmette, Ill.: Bahá'í Publishing Trust, 1977).
9. 'Abdu'l-Bahá, *Will and Testament of 'Abdu'l-Bahá* (Wilmette, Ill.: Bahá'í Publishing Trust, 1944).
10. Shoghi Effendi, *Bahá'í Administration: Selected Messages 1922-1932*, 7th rev. ed. (Wilmette, Ill.: Bahá'í Publishing Trust, 1974), p. 62.
11. Shoghi Effendi, *God Passes By*, p. 326.

THE OPENING OF THE FORMATIVE AGE
(First Epoch 1921-1944)

1. See Rúḥíyyih Rabbani, *The Priceless Pearl* (London: Bahá'í Publishing Trust, 1969), pp. 39-77.

66   Notes

2. Ibid., p. 73.
3. Shoghi Effendi, *Bahá'í Administration: Selected Messages 1922-1932*, 7th rev. ed. (Wilmette, Ill.: Bahá'í Publishing Trust, 1974), p. 26
4. Ibid., p. 34.
5. 'Abdu'l-Bahá, *Will and Testament of 'Abdu'l-Bahá* (Wilmette, Ill.: Bahá'í Publishing Trust, 1944), p. 3.
6. Very early in his Guardianship Shoghi Effendi began to sign his letters "Your true brother." He wrote, in an undated letter in 1922, "May I also express my heartfelt desire that the friends of God in every land regard me in no other light but that of a true brother, united with them in our common servitude to the Master's Sacred Threshold, and refer to me in their letters and verbal addresses always as Shoghi Effendi, for I desire to be known by no other name save the one our Beloved Master was wont to utter, a name which of all other designations is the most conducive to my spiritual growth and advancement." (*Bahá'í Administration*, p. 25).
7. Ibid., p. 42.
8. Ibid., p. 68.
9. 'Abdu'l-Bahá, quoted in George Latimer, "Message to the Bahá'ís of the West: *'Today, Whoever Is a Herald of "the Covenant", Is the Light of the Regions!'*," *Star of the West*, 5 (Nov. 23, 1914), 217.
10. See Shoghi Effendi, *Citadel of Faith: Messages to America, 1947-1957* (Wilmette, Ill.: Bahá'í Publishing Trust, 1965), pp. 30, 151, and Shoghi Effendi, *Messages to America: Selected Letters and Cablegrams Addressed to the Bahá'ís of North America, 1932-1946* (Wilmette, Ill.: Bahá'í Publishing Committee, 1947), pp. 9, 91-92, 109.
11. 'Abdu'l-Bahá, quoted in Shoghi Effendi, *The Advent of Divine Justice*, 3d rev. ed. (Wilmette, Ill.: Bahá'í Publishing Trust, 1969), p. 72.
12. Shoghi Effendi, *Citadel of Faith*, p. 34.
13. 'Abdu'l-Bahá, quoted in Shoghi Effendi, *Advent of Divine Justice*, p. 72.
14. Shoghi Effendi, *Bahá'í Administration*, p. 143.
15. Bahá'u'lláh, *Gleanings from the Writings of Bahá'u'lláh*, trans. Shoghi Effendi, 2d rev. ed. (Wilmette, Ill.: Bahá'í Publishing Trust, 1976), pp. 114, 115.
16. Shoghi Effendi, *God Passes By*, rev. ed. (Wilmette, Ill.: Bahá'í Publishing Trust, 1974), p. 366.
17. Bahá'u'lláh, *Gleanings*, pp. 110-11.
18. Shoghi Effendi, *Messages to America*, p. 3.
19. Ibid., p. 40.

20. Ibid., p. 20.
21. Shoghi Effendi, *God Passes By*, p. 386.
22. See National Spiritual Assembly of the Bahá'ís of Australia and New Zealand, "In Memoriam: John Henry Hyde Dunn," in *The Bahá'í World: A Biennial International Record, Volume IX, 1940-1944*, comp. National Spiritual Assembly of the Bahá'ís of the United States and Canada (Wilmette, Ill.: Bahá'í Publishing Committee, 1945), p. 597, and National Spiritual Assembly of the Bahá'ís of Australia, "In Memoriam: Clara Dunn: 1869-1960," in *The Bahá'í World: An International Record, Volume XIII, 1954-1963*, comp. The Universal House of Justice (Haifa: The Universal House of Justice, 1970), p. 862.
23. "In Memoriam: Marion Jack," in *The Bahá'í World: A Biennial International Record, Volume XII, 1950-1954*, comp. National Spiritual Assembly of the Bahá'ís of the United States (Wilmette, Ill.: Bahá'í Publishing Trust, 1956), p. 674.
24. "Honoring the First Pioneer to Brazil Leonora Holsapple Armstrong," *Bahá'í News*, no. 483 (June 1971), p. 6.
25. "In Memoriam: Johanna Schubarth," *Bahá'í World, Vol. XII*, p. 694.
26. Shoghi Effendi, *God Passes By*, p. 294.
27. See 'Abdu'l-Bahá, *The Bahá'í Peace Program: From the Writings of 'Abdu'l-Bahá* (New York: Bahá'í Publishing Committee, 1930). Excerpts from the Tablet to the Central Organization for a Durable Peace appear in 'Abdu'l-Bahá, in Bahá'u'lláh and 'Abdu'l-Bahá, *Bahá'í World Faith: Selected Writings of Bahá'u'lláh and 'Abdu'l-Bahá*, rev. ed. (Wilmette, Ill.: Bahá'í Publishing Trust, 1976), pp. 215-17, 284-96.
28. See H. Emogene Hoagg, "Short History of the International Bahá'í Bureau at Geneva, Switzerland," in *The Bahá'í World: A Biennial International Record, Volume IV, 1930-1932*, comp. National Spiritual Assembly of the Bahá'ís of the United States and Canada (New York: Bahá'í Publishing Committee, 1933), pp. 257-61, and Helen Bishop, "Geneva Scans the European Community," in *The Bahá'í World: A Biennial International Record, Volume VII, 1936-1938*, comp. National Spiritual Assembly of the Bahá'ís of the United States and Canada (New York: Bahá'í Publishing Committee, 1939), pp. 108-13.
29. Bahá'u'lláh, quoted in Shoghi Effendi, *The Promised Day Is Come*, rev. ed. (Wilmette, Ill.: Bahá'í Publishing Trust, 1961), p. 37.
30. Shoghi Effendi, *God Passes By*, p. 257.
31. "Dr. J. E. Esslemont," in *Bahá'í Year Book, Volume One, 1925-1926*, comp. National Spiritual Assembly of the Bahá'ís of the United States and Canada (New York: Bahá'í Publishing Committee, 1926), p. 136.

32. Helen Bishop, "A Session at the World Congress of Faiths," in *Bahá'í World, Vol. VII*, p. 635.
33. George Townshend, *The Promise of All Ages*, 3d rev. ed. (Oxford: George Ronald, 1972; Wilmette, Ill.: Bahá'í Publishing Trust, 1973).
34. Doris McKay, "In Memoriam: Martha L. Root," in *The Bahá'í World: A Biennial International Record, Volume VIII, 1938-1940*, comp. National Spiritual Assembly of the Bahá'ís of the United States and Canada (Wilmette, Ill.: Bahá'í Publishing Committee, 1942), pp. 645-46.
35. "The Passing of Bahíyyih <u>Kh</u>ánum, The Most Exalted Leaf: Passages from Tablets Revealed by 'Abdu'l-Bahá," in *The Bahá'í World: A Biennial International Record, Volume V, 1932-1934*, comp. National Spiritual Assembly of the Bahá'ís of the United States and Canada (New York: Bahá'í Publishing Committee, 1936), p. 171.
36. Shoghi Effendi, *Bahá'í Administration*, p. 194.
37. Shoghi Effendi, *God Passes By*, p. 347.
38. Shoghi Effendi, *Bahá'í Administration*, p. 191.
39. Shoghi Effendi, *The World Order of Bahá'u'lláh: Selected Letters*, 2d rev. ed. (Wilmette, Ill.: Bahá'í Publishing Trust, 1974), p. 98.
40. Shoghi Effendi, *Messages to America*, p. 33.
41. Shoghi Effendi, *Bahá'í Administration*, p. 181.
42. Ibid.
43. Shanaz Waite, "Architecture Expressing the Renewal of Religion," in *Bahá'í World, Vol. IV*, pp. 190, 193.
44. 'Abdu'l-Bahá, quoted in ibid., p. 193.
45. Henry H. Jessup, "The Religious Mission of the English Speaking Nations," in John Henry Barrows, ed., *The World's Parliament of Religions: An Illustrated and Popular Story of the World's First Parliament of Religions, Held in Chicago in Connection with the Columbian Exposition of 1893* (Chicago: The Parliament Publishing Company, 1893), II, 1126.
46. 'Abdu'l-Bahá, *The Promulgation of Universal Peace: Discourses by Abdul Baha during His Visit to the United States in 1912*, [rev. ed.] in 1 vol. (Wilmette, Ill.: Bahá'í Publishing Committee, 1943), pp. 364-65.
47. Shoghi Effendi, *Bahá'í Administration*, p. 130.
48. Shoghi Effendi, *Messages to America*, p. 1. Nabíl-i-A'ẓam [Muḥammad-i-Zarandí], *The Dawn-Breakers: Nabíl's Narrative of the Early Days of the Bahá'í Revelation*, trans. and ed. Shoghi Effendi (Wilmette, Ill.: Bahá'í Publishing Trust, 1932).

49. See Bahá'u'lláh, *The Kitáb-i-Íqán: The Book of Certitude*, trans. Shoghi Effendi, 3d ed. (Wilmette, Ill.: Bahá'í Publishing Trust, 1974); Bahá'u'lláh, *The Hidden Words of Bahá'u'lláh*, trans. Shoghi Effendi (Wilmette, Ill.: Bahá'í Publishing Trust, 1939); Bahá'u'lláh, *Gleanings from the Writings of Bahá'u'lláh*, trans. Shoghi Effendi, 2d rev. ed. (Wilmette, Ill.: Bahá'í Publishing Trust, 1976); and Bahá'u'lláh, *Prayers and Meditations*, trans. Shoghi Effendi (Wilmette, Ill.: Bahá'í Publishing Trust, 1938).

50. The first revised edition of Esslemont's *Bahá'u'lláh and the New Era* was published in 1937 under the direction of Shoghi Effendi. In 1950 the National Spiritual Assembly of the United States purchased the publishing rights to this title from Allen and Unwin, London, the original publisher. Acting under the advice of The Universal House of Justice the Bahá'í Publishing Trust in the United States published revised editions in 1970 and 1976.

51. *World Order* magazine, which had been a monthly periodical, was suspended with the March 1948 issue and was reinstated as a quarterly journal in the fall of 1966.

52. *The Bahá'í World: An International Record, Volume XIII, 1954-1963* was produced at the Bahá'í World Center under the supervision of The Universal House of Justice, which thenceforth assumed responsibility for publication of subsequent volumes.

53. Howard Colby Ives, *Portals to Freedom*, rev. ed. (London: George Ronald, 1962).

54. See Shoghi Effendi, *World Order of Bahá'u'lláh*.

55. *The Dispensation of Bahá'u'lláh* is published as a booklet (Wilmette, Ill.: Bahá'í Publishing Trust, 1934) and may also be found in *World Order of Bahá'u'lláh*, pp. 97-157.

56. *The Unfoldment of World Civilization* (New York: Bahá'í Publishing Committee, 1936) is no longer available in a booklet format but may be found in *World Order of Bahá'u'lláh*, pp. 161-206.

57. Shoghi Effendi, *Messages to America*, p. 5.

58. Ibid., p. 6.

59. Ibid., p. 8.

60. Shoghi Effendi, *Messages to the Bahá'í World: 1950-1957*, rev. ed. (Wilmette, Ill.: Bahá'í Publishing Trust, 1971), pp. 150, 44, 140.

61. Shoghi Effendi, *Messages to America*, p. 17.

62. Ibid., p. 14.

63. Shoghi Effendi, *Advent of Divine Justice*, pp. 5, 74.

64. Shoghi Effendi, *Messages to America*, p. 38.

65. Ibid., p. 40.

66. Ibid., p. 41.
67. Shoghi Effendi, *Promised Day Is Come*, p. 2.
68. Ibid., p. 129.
69. For a summary of the First Seven Year Plan see "The Seven Year Plan," in *Bahá'í World, Vol. X*, pp. 173-220.
70. See Shoghi Effendi, comp., *A World Survey of the Bahá'í Faith: 1844-1944* (Wilmette, Ill.: Bahá'í Publishing Committee, 1944).
71. Shoghi Effendi, *God Passes By*.

THE SECOND EPOCH OF THE FORMATIVE AGE
(1944-1963)

1. Shoghi Effendi, *Messages to America: Selected Letters and Cablegrams Addressed to the Bahá'ís of North America, 1932-1946* (Wilmette, Ill.: Bahá'í Publishing Committee, 1947), p. 85.
2. 'Abdu'l-Bahá, "God and the Universe: A Letter Written by 'Abdu'l-Bahá to Dr. August Forel, Switzerland, in 1921," *The Bahá'í Peace Program: From the Writings of 'Abdu'l-Bahá* (New York: Bahá'í Publishing Committee, 1930, pp. 31-47.
3. National Spiritual Assembly of the Bahá'ís of India and Burma, quoted in Horace Holley, "International Survey of Current Bahá'í Activities in the East and West," in *The Bahá'í World: A Biennial International Record, Volume XI, 1946-1950*, comp. National Spiritual Assembly of the Bahá'ís of the United States and Canada (Wilmette, Ill.: Bahá'í Publishing Committee, 1952), pp. 32-33.
4. 'Abdu'l-Bahá, *The Promulgation of Universal Peace: Discourses by Abdul Baha during His Visit to the United States in 1912*, [rev. ed.] in 1 vol. (Wilmette, Ill.: Bahá'í Publishing Committee, 1943), p. 371.
5. *The Bahá'í Peace Program* ([Wilmette, Ill.: National Spiritual Assembly of the Bahá'ís of the United States and Canada, 1945]). The pamphlet is available in a revised format from the Bahá'í Publishing Trust, Wilmette, Ill.
6. *A Bahá'í Declaration of Human Obligations and Rights: Presented to the United Nations Rights Commission*, ([Wilmette, Ill.: National Spiritual Assembly of the Bahá'ís of the United States and Canada, 1947]). A revised edition of the statement was prepared in 1960 and is available from the Bahá'í Publishing Trust, Wilmette, Ill. The text of "A Bahá'í Statement on the Rights of Women," submitted to the United Nations Commission On the Rights of Women in August 1947, was published in *World Order*, 13 (Oct. 1947), 231-32.
7. *Proposals for Charter Revision Submitted to The United Nations by*

the *Bahá'í International Community* ([n.p.: Bahá'í International Community, 1955]). *Proposals* is available from the Bahá'í Publishing Trust, Wilmette, Ill.

8. Shoghi Effendi's "The Faith of Bahá'u'lláh: A World Religion" was published in *World Order: The Bahá'í Magazine*, 13 (Oct. 1947), 219-27. It is now published by the Bahá'í Publishing Trust, Wilmette, Ill., under the same title.

9. Shoghi Effendi, *Messages to America*, pp. 97, 88.

10. Ibid., p. 88.

11. Ibid., p. 95.

12. Honor Kempton, "In Memoriam: Dagmar Dole," in *The Bahá'í World: A Biennial International Record, Volume XII, 1950-1954*, comp. National Spiritual Assembly of the Bahá'ís of the United States (Wilmette, Ill.: Bahá'í Publishing Trust, 1956), p. 702.

13. Shoghi Effendi, quoted in Horace Holley, "International Survey of Current Bahá'í Activities in the East and West," in *Bahá'í World, Vol. XI*, p. 52.

14. Shoghi Effendi, *Messages to America*, pp. 90-104.

15. Ibid., pp. 96-102, 99.

16. Ibid., p. 99. The Holy Year is discussed in Shoghi Effendi, *Messages to the Bahá'í World: 1950-1957*, rev. ed. (Wilmette, Ill.: Bahá'í Publishing Trust, 1971), pp. 17, 32-33.

17. Shoghi Effendi, *Messages to America*, pp. 100-01.

18. In 1954 the Maxwell house was transferred to the National Spiritual Assembly of the Bahá'ís of Canada as a gift from Rúḥíyyih Khánum and designated the most holy spot in Canada.

19. Shoghi Effendi, *The Challenging Requirements of the Present Hour* (Wilmette, Ill.: Bahá'í Publishing Trust, 1947). The message is now published in Shoghi Effendi, *Citadel of Faith: Messages to America, 1947-1957* (Wilmette, Ill.: Bahá'í Publishing Trust, 1965), pp. 4-38.

20. [Shoghi Effendi], *Letters from the Guardian to Australia and New Zealand: 1923-1957* ([Australia]: National Spiritual Assembly of the Bahá'ís of Australia, 1970), p. 98.

21. Ibid.

22. Shoghi Effendi, *Dawn of a New Day* (New Delhi: Bahá'í Publishing Trust, [1970]), p 151

23. Shoghi Effendi, quoted in Horace Holley, "International Survey of Current Bahá'í Activities in the East and West," in *Bahá'í World, Vol. XI*, p. 23.

24. George Townshend, *The Old Churches and the New World-Faith* (London: National Spiritual Assembly of the Bahá'ís of the British Isles,

n.d.). The essay was reprinted in *Bahá'í World, Vol. XI*, pp. 667-73.
 25. Shoghi Effendi, quoted in "International Survey of Current Bahá'í Activities: Review of Various National Events—Persia," *Bahá'í World, Vol. XII*, p. 65.
 26. Shoghi Effendi, *Messages to the Bahá'í World*, p. 169.
 27. Shoghi Effendi, *Citadel of Faith*, p. 87.
 28. The Universal House of Justice, quoted in Amín Banání, "Músá Banání: 1886-1971," in *The Bahá'í World: An International Record, Volume XV, 1968-1973*, comp. The Universal House of Justice (Haifa: Bahá'í World Centre, 1975), p. 421.
 29. Shoghi Effendi, *Messages to America*, p. 80.
 30. Shoghi Effendi, *Messages to the Bahá'í World*, p. 28.
 31. Ibid., pp. 7-8.
 32. 'Abdu'l-Bahá, *Will and Testament of 'Abdu'l-Bahá* (Wilmette, Ill.: Bahá'í Publishing Trust, 1944), pp. 13, 12.
 33. Shoghi Effendi, "No Respite in Bahá'í Activity during World Crusade," *Bahá'í News*, no. 257 (Jul. 1952), p. 2.
 34. *Launching the World-Embracing Spiritual Crusade* was published as an insert to *Bahá'í News*, no. 261 (Nov. 1952); it is now published in Shoghi Effendi, *Messages to the Bahá'í World*, pp. 40-45.
 35. Ibid., p. 44.
 36. Ibid., p. 153.
 37. Ibid.
 38. Ibid., p. 41.
 39. Ibid., p. 74.
 40. Shoghi Effendi, *Citadel of Faith*, p. 106.
 41. See Shoghi Effendi, *Messages to the Bahá'í World*, pp. 49, 50-53, 55.
 42. Clara Dunn, quoted in "The Asian Intercontinental Teaching Conference Held in New Delhi, India, October 7-15, 1953: (2) Report of the Asian Intercontinental Teaching Conference," in *Bahá'í World, Vol. XII*, p. 184.
 43. [Shoghi Effendi], *The Bahá'í Faith: 1844-1952* (Wilmette, Ill.: Bahá'í Publishing Committee, 1953).
 44. Dhikru'lláh Khádem, quoted in "The European Intercontinental Teaching Conference Held in Stockholm, Sweden, July 21-26, 1953: (2) Report of the European Intercontinental Teaching Conference," in *Bahá'í World, Vol. XII*, p. 173.
 45. Shoghi Effendi, *Messages to the Bahá'í World*, p. 101.
 46. Ibid., pp. 101-02.
 47. The map entitled "Progress Bahá'í World Crusade 1953-1958" is

included as an insert in *The Bahá'í World: An International Record, Volume XIII, 1954-1963*, comp. The Universal House of Justice (Haifa: The Universal House of Justice, 1970).
48. Shoghi Effendi, *Messages to the Bahá'í World*, p. 122.
49. Ibid., p. 127.
50. Ibid., p. 130.
51. 'Abdu'l-Bahá, *Will and Testament*, p. 3.
52. From a new translation of the Tablet of the World.
53. See Shoghi Effendi, *Messages to the Bahá'í World*, pp. 7-8, and "Third Annual Message From the Hands of the Cause To the Bahá'ís of East and West," *Bahá'í News*, no. 346 (Dec. 1959), p. 2.
54. 'Abdu'l-Bahá, *Will and Testament*, p. 14.
55. Shoghi Effendi, *Messages to the Bahá'í World*, pp. 153, 8.
56. Ibid., p. 8.
57. For references to the epochs in the Divine Plan and in the Formative Age see Shoghi Effendi, *Messages to the Bahá'í World*, pp. 8, 16, 19, 31, 41, 58, 61, 144, 154, and Shoghi Effendi, *Messages to America*, pp. 89, 101.
58. The Universal House of Justice, *Wellspring of Guidance: Messages, 1963-1968*, 1st rev. ed. (Wilmette, Ill.: Bahá'í Publishing Trust, 1976), pp. 1, 2.
59. By late 1957 arrangements had been made for eleven National Spiritual Assemblies to have branches in the Holy Land, legally entitled to hold property, and recognized by the State of Israel, thus achieving a goal set by Shoghi Effendi for the World Crusade.
60. The Universal House of Justice, *Wellspring of Guidance*, p. 3.

THE THIRD EPOCH OF THE FORMATIVE AGE

1. Shoghi Effendi, *Messages to the Bahá'í World: 1950-1957*, rev. ed. (Wilmette, Ill.: Bahá'í Publishing Trust, 1971), pp. 153-55.
2. The Universal House of Justice, *Wellspring of Guidance: Messages, 1963-1968*, 1st rev. ed. (Wilmette, Ill.: Bahá'í Publishing Trust, 1976), pp. 22-27.
3. Ibid., p. 38.
4. Shoghi Effendi, *Citadel of Faith: Messages to America, 1947-1957* (Wilmette, Ill.: Bahá'í Publishing Trust, 1965), p. 117.
5. The Universal House of Justice, *Wellspring of Guidance*, pp. 96, 92.
6. Ibid., p. 109.

7. Bahá'u'lláh, *The Proclamation of Bahá'u'lláh to the Kings and Leaders of the World* (Haifa: Bahá'í World Centre, 1967).
8. Shoghi Effendi, *God Passes By*, rev. ed. (Wilmette, Ill.: Bahá'í Publishing Trust, 1974), p. 171.
9. The Universal House of Justice, *Wellspring of Guidance*, p. 120.
10. *The Bahá'í Faith: Statistical Information 1844-1968 Including the Current Status of the Goals of the Nine Year International Teaching Plan 1964-1973* ([Haifa, Israel]: The Universal House of Justice, 1968).
11. "The Travels of Amatu'l-Bahá Rúhíyyih Khánum during the Nine Year Plan," in *The Bahá'í World: An International Record, Volume XV, 1968-1973*, comp. The Universal House of Justice (Haifa: Bahá'í World Centre, 1975), p. 605.
12. Ibid.
13. The Universal House of Justice, quoted in ibid., p. 588.
14. The Universal House of Justice, *Messages from The Universal House of Justice: 1968-1973* (Wilmette, Ill.: Bahá'í Publishing Trust, 1976), pp. 69, 72.
15. Ibid., p. 113.
16. Ibid., pp. 118, 117.
17. Ibid., p. 105.
18. His Highness Malietoa Tanumafili II, quoted in "First Head of State Embraces the Cause of Bahá'u'lláh," in *Bahá'í World, Vol. XV*, p. 183.
19. The Universal House of Justice, "International Teaching Centre Established in Holy Land," *Bahá'í News*, no. 508 (Jul. 1973), p. 1.
20. Ibid.
21. Shoghi Effendi, *Bahá'í Administration: Selected Messages 1922-1932*, 7th rev. ed. (Wilmette, Ill.: Bahá'í Publishing Trust, 1974), pp. 50, 52.
22. The Universal House of Justice, *Messages*, pp. 119-20.